FLOAT FISHING: RIVERS

Ken Giles
and
Dave Harrell

Compiled and Edited by Dave King

Beekay Publishers

Other angling titles by Beekay Publishers

Coarse

Carp Fever by Kevin Maddocks
The Art of Pole Fishing by Dickie Carr
Pike Fishing in the 80's by Neville Fickling
Basic Carp Fishing by Peter Mohan
Modern Specimen Hunting by Jim Gibbinson
Top Ten—tactics for the major species from ten leading anglers
Edited by Bruce Vaughan
Redmire Pool by Kevin Clifford & Len Arbery
Tactics for Big Pike by Bill Chillingworth
In Pursuit of Carp & Catfish by Kevin Maddocks
Cypry the Carp by Peter Mohan
The Beekay Guide to 450 Carp Waters
Jim Davidson Gets Hooked by Jim Davidson
In Pursuit of Predatory Fish by Neville Fickling
Tiger Bay by Rob Maylin
Understanding Barbel by Fred Crouch
Big-Water Carp by Jim Gibbinson
Mega-Pike by Eddie Turner

Sea

Boat Fishing at Sea by Phill Williams & Brian Douglas
Long Range Casting & Fishing Techniques by Paul Kerry
Cod Fishing by John Rawle
Uptide & Boatcasting by Bob Cox

Game

The Colour Guide to Fly-Tying by Kevin Hyatt
Robson's Guide to Stillwater Trout Flies by Kenneth Robson
Dressed to Kill by Bob Carnill & Kenneth Robson

First published in 1990 by
BEEKAY PUBLISHERS
WITHY POOL, BEDFORD ROAD,
HENLOW CAMP, BEDS. SG16 6EA

© Beekay Publishers 1990

ISBN 0 947674 23 3

Typeset by BP Integraphics Ltd., Bath, Avon
Printed in Great Britain at The Bath Press, Avon

Contents

INTRODUCTION by Dave King   5

PROFILE: Ken Giles   7

PROFILE: Dave Harrell   9

THE SHAKESPEARE SUPERTEAM   11

RODS AND REELS   15

LINE AND HOOKS   23

FLOATS   29

FISHING THE STICK FLOAT   33

FISHING THE WAGGLER   45

OTHER METHODS   59

FEEDING METHODS AND TACTICS   65

MATCH EXPERIENCES   85

Introduction

By Dave King

No competitive sport has seen as many dramatic changes to its basic format, its equipment and variety in winning methods than match angling has seen over the last decade. The 1980's has seen the advent and the development of sponsored teams with semi-professional attitudes and uniformed regalia appearing at all levels of the sport and an exchange of information through the angling press and in books and articles that would have been unthinkable in the 1960's and 70's.

Any angler has freely available to him the latest equipment and information needed to become a successful match angler. The only thing that cannot be purchased is experience and confidence. This can only be obtained the hard way, by dedication, commitment and hard work.

You need these qualities to succeed in any sport, and whilst many sports are unpredictable, none are more so than match fishing. If an athlete is in good form and does everything right on the day, then some sort of measured success will normally be assured. Not so with match angling, at least not 100% of the time. But not every failure can be blamed on the draw bag, as much as we would like to think it can. We still have, at all levels of the sport, be it at club, local association, or open match fishing level, where, as a general rule, the top 10% of anglers catch 90% of the fish. Why do the same small group of top teams and individuals always seem to end up in the finals of the national winter and summer leagues? Can it be that they are all as consistently lucky? I think not.

Mix amongst these top teams at any top level match draw and one thing will be immediately apparent. They all exude a quiet confidence and self assurance. They know the 'method' for the day and have the confidence to see it through. Some will have a good day, for others nothing will go right, but they are used to taking the knocks as well as reaping the rewards, but at the same time learning by them.

Most of the functions they will perform during the match will be done mechanically, without conscious thought. All aspects of tackle handling will be completely mastered, leaving the mind free to concentrate upon what is happening below the surface and to get the maximum potential out of the peg. The equipment they use will be of the highest quality, but it will have been kept as simple as possible, as will the rigs being used. Contrary to popular belief, the top anglers do not have secret floats, or magic shotting patterns. Over complication and the chasing of rainbows is left to the other 90% of the field, as will be revealed in this book.

I must say that I went into these interviews with many preconceived ideas, but came out of them a chastened and wiser man. The revelations were not what I expected, but upon analysing them the answers could not be anything else. I mean, common sense and the ability to see the obvious are not normally considered to be 'closely guarded secrets'. But these turned out to be the jewels in the crown of these interviews, much to my surprise and delight. I can now throw out 90% of the theory that has been cluttering my head and holding me back for this last 20 years and concentrate on the 10% of real issues that will hopefully improve my performance beyond measure. Ken Giles summed it up in the very first chapter with regards to rods and which applies to everything else as well: that 'most anglers tend to complicate what is really a very simple issue'. It is not tackle that makes a good angler, but the way a good angler makes the tackle work. Providing the equipment is designed to do the job properly, it is up to the angler as to how well he performs with it. The largest chapter in this book is concerned not with equipment, but with feeding tactics. These are the real keys to success. Before we can catch a fish we must attract it into the swim and induce it to take the bait. Once this has been achieved, we then need to continue this process more efficiently than the next man with an equal opportunity, and with regards to the conditions prevailing. We will make mistakes, even top anglers make mistakes, but they do not make them quite so often, and when they do they identify them far more quickly and rectify the situation with the minimum of effect to their final result.

When I took on the commission to write this series of books and The Shakespeare Superteam agreed to these no-holds-barred interviews, I knew I had the chance to produce something really special. I was determined on behalf of myself and the other 90% of lesser mortals not to blow it, and not to come away with a missed opportunity. As to the final result, only you the reader can judge. I feel that by keeping the interviews in the format of how they actually went, as opposed to re-hashing them into normal book form, I have kept the authoritative sincerity of the anglers concerned with regards to both content and fact. If your overall approach is transformed as much as mine has been after reading it, then I feel I will have succeeded. Best wishes and tight lines.

Profile: Ken Giles

Ken Giles has been an angler for as long as he can remember. He was introduced to the sport and encouraged in his youth by his uncle, Tom Ryder from Leigh in Lancashire, the home of course of Benny and Kevin Ashurst, two of angling's greatest exponents, whose influence rubbed off on Ken via his uncle, who was also a good match angler in his own right.

After completing his National Service in the late 1950's, Ken started his match fishing apprenticeship at the age of 21. Very few anglers at that time had their own transport, relying on club coach trips to get around to the main match venues outside the local area. Ken joined a number of local clubs, ensuring that he would be fishing a club match most weekends and covered a wide variety of venues gaining in technique and experience all of the time. Eventually he worked his way through the trial match system used at that time by Birmingham A.A. to select their All England team. In 1961, at the age of 25, he became the youngest angler ever to qualify and fish for Birmingham in the National Championships, a position he kept until Birmingham A.A. dropped out of the N.F.A. Ken then moved to the Coleshill team and continued to fish the National Championships at division 1 level until 5 years ago.

At this time one of his clubs, Gleveum were dropping out of the National Championships due to lack of funds and Ken offered to help them continue in the event and make it self-financing, providing they agreed to allow him to select and manage the team. This was agreed and in the last 5 years Ken has taken his team from Division 5 to Division 1, an incredible record. Despite his individual success over the years, which has included 3 England Caps in the World Championships, the Woodbine Championships and other notable successes too numerous to mention, Ken now finds team success far more rewarding than individual achievement and it is here that he now successfully concentrates his efforts.

Profile: Dave Harrell

Dave started fishing at the age of 5, enjoying regular outings with his father and grandfather. He took up match fishing at the age of 16, building up his experience in that first year to annihilate the opposition in his second year by winning all of the club's matches in that season. The following season, at the age of 18, he joined the Amery Club in Willinghall near Walsall which gave him the big step up into Open Match fishing. After gaining in both experience and confidence and with several notable individual successes whilst a member of several smaller match groups in the Birmingham area, he was invited to join the Starlets match group in 1982, and was a member of their Captain Morgan Cup winning side in 1983.

Now an experienced all-round angler, having won many open events on rivers, still-waters and canals, his invitation to join the Shakespeare Superteam came in 1984, and he has only missed one team selection in the last six years, and says that was down to his own fault.

He was called up to represent England in the Home International in 1987 and his ultimate ambition is to fish for England in the World Championships.

In 1989 he became the Angler's Mail Matchman of the Year and narrowly missed out last season (1989–90) on repeating this success. I feel certain that, but for the rivers being unfishable during the closing weeks of the season, this achievement would have been repeated. He will certainly be the man to beat this year. Now, at the age of 32, he is intending to join that small group of elite professional anglers and make match angling his full-time career. I am certain that with his undisputed ability and single-minded approach and confidence, he will succeed and continue to go from strength to strength and fulfil his ultimate ambition.

Notable Individual Successes
1978:—Walsall Champion
1981:—Avon Team Championships: Individual Winner
1983:—W. B. Clarke's Businessmens Champion (Stourport)

1984:—Evesham League Champion
1987:—Birmingham Angling Festival Champion (Edgbaston)
1988:—West Midlands Winter League Champion
        John Smiths Champion
        Twyford League Champion
        River Colebrook Champion (Ireland)
        Lewis Businessmens Champion (Stourport)
1989:—Wychavon Champion (Evesham)
        Anglers Mail Matchman of the Year
1990:—W. B. Clarke's Businessmens Champion (River Avon)

The Shakespeare Superteam

The name 'The Shakespeare Superteam' needs very little introduction to anyone who knows and partakes in the sport of match fishing. Since their formation they have always been the team to beat if success is to be assured and have always been at the forefront of angling achievement. Their consistency has always been based upon having the cream of current angling talent amid their ranks, and this being encouraged and directed to its full potential by the team manager and captain Ken Giles. The strength of the team lies in the fact that it consists of a strong and resolute core of individual anglers. This may sound like a contradiction of terms, but Ken is certain that this quality of individualism is what makes them so consistent as a team. Their general all-round ability, combined with their individual approach to the various methods required to be utilised under a variety of conditions, is what makes up their awesome collective strength. Over the years, names have changed and new talent has been brought forward and encouraged, ensuring a continuity in results virtually unequalled in match fishing history. Team championships and competitions are a development of the last decade and will be at the forefront of angling in the future whatever that future may bring. The days of the secretive individual were numbered once the format of the old 'All England Championships' was altered from an individual and team weight, to a team points system. Professionalism has now taken over and no team typifies this approach more than the Superteam. Under the banner of Gleveum A.C. they have risen through each of the divisions annually to achieve their rightful place in Division one of the N.F.A. Championships and it is only a matter of time before the title of Division One Champions is assured.

I will now let Ken take over and tell the story of the team's conception and what he considers to be the key to its success.

Ken: In 1973, Clive Smith and myself approached various tackle companies with a view to financial sponsorship. At that time this had never been done before and was a totally new concept with regards to angling. A few top anglers had, in the past, associated themselves with tackle companies and put their names to various products, but no one had approached anyone with regards to actual cash sponsorship to represent the company on the match circuit.

Most of them laughed us off and said that this sort of thing can never happen, but one company, Shakespeare, did not dismiss us out of hand. We had a couple of meetings with them and they did show some interest. They saw that Clive and myself were getting fairly consistent results and they saw that there could be something in it for the benefit of the promotion of the company and, of course, for Clive and myself.

In the end they decided to sponsor us and in return we were given a free hand in the development and design of specific products for the match angler and these became very successful. The Match International range of rods and reels became very popular and out-sold any other companies Match fishing products during this period.

Up to this time, major angling matches and events were tailored to individual weight performance and what few team events there were also concentrated on total weight to decide the outcome.

Apart from the National Championships, these were mainly aimed at four-man teams, and would run a four-man team prize as a supplement to the major prize which was aimed at individual performance. Again these would be decided on a total weight basis, but each man would draw as an individual. At this time there were no sectional draws for the team event.

To try to make our mark under the system as it stood, we were allowed to recruit two more members into the sponsorship arrangement with a view to entering the team events. These two were Max Winters and Tony Davis.

This lasted for several years and we were quite successful as both a team and as individuals.

Eventually, due to the increased interest and publicity generated by the success of ourselves and other teams such as the Leicester Likely Lads and the Starlets etc., team events became more popular and in some top events these were expanded for teams of six. To be able to take part in these and also to give ourselves a pool from which to field a four-man team regardless of illness, holidays etc., we recruited another two anglers: Dave Williams and Steve Webb.

Currently, only three of the original six are still fishing. As most people know, Clive, sadly died, and Max Winters and Dave Williams have both since given up fishing totally. This was a great loss to angling, but unfortunately these things inevitably happen.

By this time, team fishing as we know it now, was rapidly being developed. The introduction of the points system in the National Championships was adopted for the winter and summer league events and many of these now catered for teams of up to twelve anglers. Due to the success we had achieved, and the effect this had on tackle development and sales, the Shakespeare Company allowed us to expand our squad to its present level of fourteen anglers, from which a strong team of twelve can be selected at any one time, with regards to current form and strengths on each particular venue. It also helps with things such as holidays and work commitments, occasional health or family problems etc. If we only had twelve members and due to a car breaking down or sudden illness we were a man short on the day, as a team we would be dead. So by having a squad of fourteen we can always be certain in a twelve-man event of fielding a strong team.

There have been a number of changes over the years. For various reasons anglers have lost form, or due to working or matrimonial pressures, have been unable to maintain their commitment to the sport and it is my job as Captain and Manager to maintain the continuity and strength within the squad. All the squad members are very experienced, successful individual anglers within their own right, but when we fish as a team they are committed team anglers.

The selection of the team on the day is my decision alone. None of the team are consulted or need to be concerned with team selection. There are times when I have the unpleasant job of telling a team member he is dropped, due to lack of form etc., but my decision is always unquestionably accepted and with good spirit. This policy is, I feel, the best for the moral of the team in the long term. I do not agree with systems where teams are decided by selection of a committee or by consultation. If that same enthusiasm was shown on the river bank as is shown around a bar when discussing and selecting team members, these teams would win everything going. Instead I think they are negative and divisive.

Such is our relationship and commitment that I rarely have to make the decision to drop an angler for a particular match. If, due to loss of form or any other reason, any of the lads feel he should be dropped for a particular match, he will normally approach me with this view in mind, as opposed to me approaching him. Should this happen, I know I can still count upon him turning up on the day, if asked, to run the bank and give us 110% effort in collating and passing on the necessary information to the team.

One of our greatest strengths is that our team consists of a majority of mature anglers who are settled in their life-styles and have the full support of their families and employers. This is essential if you are to give the degree of commitment necessary to succeed. Many anglers can do this over a period of two or three years, but to maintain this over a period of ten or twelve years, despite the pitfalls that they will inevitably come up against, means that these men are exceptional. They are something special and I am proud to have anglers of this calibre in the team. They are the key to our continual success.

Rods and Reels

Q. *Which types of rods do you prefer for the various aspects of float fishing on rivers and what qualities do you find important?*

Ken: The choice of rod tends to be a very personal thing and this is reflected to some extent by the vast range now available on the market. Years ago, I started out using split cane, and then moved on to glass fibre. In the glass era, the popular length was around 12 ft. The reason for this was, that due to the nature of the material being used, 12 ft was an ideal length.

Now, with the use of carbon, boron and kevlar etc, the rods are getting progressively slimmer and lighter, without any reduction in strength or action and now most match float rods are 13 ft–14 ft long.

As I have already said, rods are very personal things. Some people make short butts to fit 13 ft rods to reduce them down for if they get pegged under trees etc, but generally most match rods are between 13ft and 14 ft and again, personally, over the past 5 or 6 years I have used boron. But lately I have been converted to the Shakespeare Victory X kevlar. Now I'm not trying to plug it, but you have asked me what I personally use. What I have done with mine is, I have scraped it down and re-rung it with hard chrome rings, as opposed to using it with the lined rings which are fitted as standard by the factory and I normally carry two identical 13 ft rods with me plus two extra butt sections. One of these butts will reduce them down to 12 ft and the other will extend them up to 14 ft in length and these meet all of the float fishing situations I am likely to come up against in this country for use with stick float or waggler, on rivers or still waters. The tips I prefer are always spliced and a lot of rubbish has been written in the past about the need for one type of tip for this and another type for that. Top anglers, like any other top sportsmen who use hand held equipment, such as snooker and tennis players etc, need to know that when they take hold of their cue, racket or rod, they can make it perform. There is something built in to a top angler who handles the same rod all of the time, that lets them

Don't forget — discarded line kills birds and other wild animals

instinctively know how to get the best from that rod, be it casting or striking etc. They know how to cushion the strike within the limitations of whichever hook length they are using, they know how to get the maximum casting distance when required, they know how to successfully play and land quality fish on fine tackle. All of these things they can do instinctively and you have just got to give these anglers a little bit of credit for their ability to read any given situation. An example of what I am talking about: you may be watching a top class angler fishing in a strong down stream wind. On occasions he will give an almighty strike and you think 'My God, he's cracked off', then suddenly you will see the rod take on a curve as he starts playing a fish. What you fail to realise is, that he has done this thousands of times before, with the same rod in similar conditions. He knows exactly how much the line has bowed and what power he needs to put into the strike to pick up that line and connect with the fish, at the same time cushioning it so that he doesn't crack off. What looks like a wild strike to you is to him a perfectly controlled strike to beat the conditions prevailing.

If I were to be using one type of rod for this and another type for that, I would lose this very personal control and confidence that I gain by using the same tool all of the time and making it work under all float fishing situations.

Dave: For my part, for most of the fishing I do, using floats from two to two and a half swan shot capacity, I carry three identical 13 ft spliced tip rods with me and use them for all my fishing in this country. But when I go over to Ireland, where I may be using 3 or 4 swan capacity floats and heavier hook lengths, which is a situation that doesn't occur very often in this country, then a spliced tip is too fine for this and I would be looking to using a stronger straight taper tip, such as that supplied as an alternative top with the Shakespeare Victory X kevlar. Normally, in this country, if you come up against situations requiring the use of floats heavier than two and a half swan, you would switch from the float to the swimfeeder anyway.

So for general match fishing where you are also using 22–24 hooks and ¾ lb bottoms, a spliced tip is absolutely vital to provide a cushioning effect and to prevent cracking off.

I use hard chrome rings on all three of my rods, in line with the trend in the Midlands area. I don't know exactly why this is, but I have tried using rods with lined rings and I cannot get on with them. But having said that, you go down south and everyone is using rods with lined rings!

Ken: Dave is one hundred per cent right on this. The use of hard chrome rings is Midlands orientated and yet when you go down south it's got to be lined rings. The reason is I think, that when you buy a £150.00 rod and you have got not cheap, but good quality hard chrome rings on it, it does not look as good or as well finished as a rod with lined rings. Also, the main selling point is of course, that a rod with lined rings will never wear out, whereas the hard chrome rings will need replacing every season. So naturally the demand from the average angler is for lined rings. But of course, very few newcomers have ever used rods with hard chrome rings, so they do not realise the advantages gained by their qualities of reduced friction when casting and running through etc, which makes the hassle of replacing them every now and again so worthwhile.

Dave: One final point from me on that one: I have always found it very important to carry around a number of float rods that are identical. I've always done it ever since I first started going around the match circuit. At that time, I used to use Match Internationals which were, in my opinion, the best of the glass fibre match rods. Most of the rods I have used since have been based upon that type of action and as Ken has already said, although they have got progressively slimmer and lighter they have still kept those classic Match International qualities.

But it is very important whichever type of action you prefer, to have a number of identical rods, because you get to know the qualities of the rod and as Ken has already mentioned, when you need to pick up twenty or thirty yards of line whilst using ¾ lb, or on occasions even finer bottoms, you must know the qualities and the limitations of the rod if you are not going to be continually cracking off and losing fish, which lets face it, no match angler can afford to do.

This is only something you can get used to over the course of time by using one particular type of rod, so by having 2 or 3 rods the same it is comforting to know that if during the course of a match, you do need to pick up a rod with a different rig, that it is an exact duplicate and it is going to perform exactly the same and you know its qualities and limitations.

Ken: There are only so many 'thinking' anglers in every thousand that go fishing. As Dave has already said, he only uses one type of rod and carries 3 identical rods to do all his float fishing with. He has totally thought it through and his experience over the years has confirmed that this approach is the right one. The other 900 and odd non-thinking anglers read in the articles and in the manufacturer's catalogues that you need this for stick float fishing and you need that for waggler fishing etc and it just isn't so. I know we seem to keep going on and on about this, but when you try to explain to them that the really successful anglers who have thought it through, only carry 2 or 3 identical rods to cover

Fig. 1. Rod actions: spliced tip and straight taper.

all of their float fishing requirements they just do not believe it! They still think they need a stick float rod and a waggler rod etc and here's Dave, who over the last few years is probably the most successful angler in England, using 3 identical rods for everything. So who is right? Him, or the hundreds of less successful anglers who are complicating what is really a very simple issue.

Q. *Well, that should certainly give a lot of people food for thought. Let us now go on to reels. Which types of reels do you use for trotting and what features do you find essential?*

Dave: This is where you will find we differ greatly. I still favour the use of close face reels. I've tried to use open spool reels and I do in fact use them for heavy line fishing. For instance, if I am fishing on the river Severn, the Middle Severn in particular, the float fishing on there does call for the use of 3 and 4 lb mainlines, and closed face reels just do not lend themselves to the use of heavy lines. But for general float fishing with 2 lb–2.5 lb lines, then for me it has got to be closed face reels. I have tried to switch over and I can successfully use open faced reels, but not as confidently as I do when using closed face reels. I tend to favour the Abu 507. Unfortunately it was a reel that they stopped making about ten years ago and although since then there have been many attempts to imitate it, no one in my opinion has come up with a reel that is as good. I have 6 of these, 3 that I always carry and 3 in reserve for if they ever breakdown or get stolen. I was fortunate a few years ago in being able to buy the ones I have got now in a closing down sale and I have such confidence in them that I bought every one that he had. Over the course of time I have noticed, again in the West Midlands area, anglers are switching back to using closed face reels and this particular model, although no longer available now, is in great demand and anglers are scouring the country looking for good second hand models.

I have had a set of very shallow spools made up for me that take only 40 to 60 yards of 2 lb line. I use the 40 yard spools for stick float fishing and the 60 yards spools for waggler fishing and the only other modification I have made is to remove the anti-reverse mechanism from the inside. I find that these reels cover 90% of my fishing on flowing water. It is important to change the line regularly. I always change mine every 3 weeks or 6 outings. I do think that this is essential.

I change the pick up pin on the reels about twice a season because they do tend to wear and only other thing I do is give them a good dowsing of W.D. 40 every 2 or 3 months. They do sound like a bag of nails sometimes when I'm using them and some people do quip that it is time I changed the B.B. shot inside them, but the noise does not bother me and if it puts other anglers off, all well and good. Despite the noise, they are very smooth and the pull of a fish can easily backwind them, which is of course another great advantage.

Ken: I'm the opposite, I prefer to use the open faced reel, but having said that I do carry and sometimes use a closed faced reel. They are very handy when fishing in a strong wind or heavy rain, etc, when open faced reels are prone to tangling, also they are useful in fast fishing situations when you have a shoal of dace in front of you and the one handed push button action does speed up your casting. But generally, I prefer to use open spool reels and the type I like for float fishing are the 035 Shakespeare graphite. These are nice reels, they are light and smooth and you can backwind with no problems at all. An important feature of these reels is the facility to manually close the bail arm. This is a very important feature for a trotting reel. I never have liked the idea of closing the bail arm after hooking a fish by turning the handle to engage it. You are not in control and many a fish has been lost at this point. By being able to close the bail arm manually you are always in control and as the reel also turns the 'right way' the pick up takes the line off of your finger without allowing any slack to occur.

Again, as with rods, reel preference can tend to be a personal thing. Dave prefers his closed face reels and he thinks he is right, I prefer my open spools reels and I am convinced I am right, the important thing is that you have total confidence in what you use.

Dave: There is one point I would like to make here, which sums up this difference in preference. Many top anglers I know, still prefer to use the Mitchell Match. Now this is a reel I have never been able to get on with. For a start the head turns the 'wrong way'. Whenever I pick up a rod with a Mitchell Match reel on I experience all sorts of problems, but many top anglers use them and make them work.

One other point that I feel is worth mentioning. One of the main reasons that Ken doesn't get on with using the close face reel is that for him the line sometimes seem to bed in on the spool and not run off as smoothly as it does off of the wider spool of the open type. I don't notice this because I always tend to feed the line off the spool by hand anyway, whether stick float or waggler fishing, so it all comes back again to personal style; what suits one person is totally unacceptable to another. The important thing is to try the different styles and settle upon the one that works for you and then stick to it.

Ken: Yes I agree with that. The important thing is to have confidence in what you use, but at the same time you must be prepared to make the change when conditions dictate it, and although we do use different reels most of the time, we each realise when to change and when it is to our advantage to use another method.

Another point I would like to make is that many of the reels now coming onto the market are to me, totally unsuitable for trotting. In many cases they are too big and heavy, but most important of all, they have too higher a gear ratio. The worst thing that can happen when you are trotting down a river is to get line twist. The number of times you see anglers retrieving their tackle at high speed and as they lift the bait out of the water it is spinning like a top. This is no good at all.

When this happens you have no alternative but to break your hook-length off and start again. Because no matter what else you do, once that spin starts to happen you will be plagued by it for the rest of the session. So, high speed retrieve serves no purpose whatsoever. One of the beauties of using a centrepin reel was, that due to its lack of gearing and slow retrieve, this line twist never used to happen and I know this must sound confusing in a sport where speed generally is essential, but in the long term, fast retrieve is a disadvantage and will give you nothing but problems.

Dave: I quite agree, it seemed several years ago that manufacturers were having a competition between themselves, to see who could produce the highest gearing. One of the other attractions I find with my old 507's, is that the gear ratio is very low, so I have more feel through the reel when playing a fish and I never get plagued with line twist. This is just another example of people jumping on to the fashion bandwagon without properly thinking things out.

One of the most commonly asked questions I get from anglers concerns line twist and I am sure that 90% of the problem lies with the speed of retrieve.

Line and Hooks

Q. *We all have different preferences in the brands and types of lines we use for various types of fishing. What qualities do you look for in lines for stick float fishing and how do they differ, if at all, when choosing a line for waggler fishing?*

Dave: Again there was a trend not so long ago when anglers were talking about using different lines for use with the stick float, or the waggler and using different makes and different thicknesses for each job.

Personally I use the same brand for both and this is Shakespeare Omni and I carry 2 lb and 2.5 lb on my reels. It is a good line and my results must surely confirm this. It is fairly supple, floats well, which as I will be explaining later is important, but on those occasions when I do need to sink it below the surface I can cut it under quite easily without it sinking down through the water too far, which for float fishing on rivers is an essential quality.

It is important when buying your line to use a micrometer to measure its diameter. Despite manufacturer's claims, lines do vary in diameter and spools do get wrongly labelled and there is nothing more frustrating than seeing your tackle go down the river on its own because what you thought was a 2 lb line turns out to be only 1.5 lb.

For reference purposes a good 2 lb breaking strain line must be ·0055″ in thickness, which in laymen's terms is 5½ thou' and a 2.5 lb line must be 6 thou'. Now you go through the different brands and you find for example that 1.5 lb Maxima is exactly the same diameter as 2 lb Omni, so it stands to reason that it is really 2 lb breaking strain and if you put it to the test you will find that this is correct, so it is very important if you are to get the balance of your main line and hooklength correct, that you must measure your lines. I won't touch upon the double strength lines at this stage because they are something I do not have much faith in for running line fishing.

For hooklengths I obviously use much finer lines and I use Force in the lower breaking strains such as ½ lb and ¾ lb and for 1 lb and

Please remember — litter loses fishing

1.5 lb I use Omni. These are 3 thou'–3½ thou', 4 thou' and 4½ thou', respectively, so as you see I have a perfect balance all the way down and if I should break off at all, it will always be on the hooklength.

As I have already mentioned, it is important when river fishing to use a good floating line. Omni, as I have mentioned is a good line, as is Bayer who have just brought out a 2 lb line which is also good, then there is Tortue, which again is popular. These are all good lines for float fishing on rivers. But it is also important, regardless of which brand of line you use, to use them in conjunction with a silicon spray. This is something else which has caught on in recent years and it does make a big difference. I always spray it on my spool before the start and even if the wind does get up later on, I find I can still sink the line when I have to and then leave it on the surface again if the wind drops.

In conjunction with this I also use Mucilin or Vaseline on the line immediately above the float. This is also very important. It is always this last 3 or 4 feet of line which is the most difficult to control without pulling your tackle off line and by greasing it, you can lift it off of the surface much more easily, mending the line right down to the float. It also prevents it from sinking, which it is prone to do if left untreated, making it almost impossible to control.

Ken: I've got to be a 'Yes' man on this, as I completely agree. Lines do vary from batch to batch and you have got to mic. it up. By doing this you are leaving nothing to chance and once you've got it right your confidence will be sky high, knowing that nothing silly is going to go wrong.

With regards to spraying the line, it is so important and now with the introduction of the silicon sprays it is made so easy. When I think of the lengths we had to go to to achieve this years ago, you modern anglers don't realise you have been born!

With regard to double strength lines. I have had a bit to do with these lines over the last couple of years and the main advantage of them is that for a given breaking strain, because of the lower diameter, they are much more supple than standard lines and as we have already pointed out, for river fishing that can be a disadvantage, mainly because this very suppleness makes them prone to twisting. They do have their applications in the higher breaking strains, or for still water fishing and pole fishing, but for use in running water they do have their limitations.

Q.   *What hook patterns and sizes do you use for the various species and baits and how would these vary to suit changing conditions?*

Ken: It's a big subject this and again it's very personal, I can only tell you what I use and how this came about. For 60 to 70% of my fishing

I use the Mustad 90340 barbless. Having said that, they are not the same as the original pattern that first came out in the 70's and despite what the manufacturers say, the pattern has been changed and they are not as good as they were. They are shorter in every respect. But let me start at the beginning. I went to France and I bought some 90340's in 16's, 18's and 20's to use specifically for bleak fishing, because at that time there was a lot of bleak in the rivers and matches were being won on them. When I got them home I tried them out and I found that they were no good at all for bleak. For some reason most of the bleak were landing in the field behind me and I was forever having to get up off of my basket to pick the wretched things up, but I did find that they were superb for catching other fish. At that time I knew a chap called Harold Greenaway and he offered to get me some more of these hooks from Mustad. He got me some of those long boxes containing several thousand packed in white boxes of 100 and I got a box of each size 20's, 18's and 16's. As you can imagine these lasted me a long time. And when I told people that I used barbless, no one believed me and I was thought of as a fake so, I kept my mouth closed and I just kept on using them. Gradually their use became accepted and when I won the Woodbine, everyone wanted barbless hooks and before long all the shops were sold out. When eventually my stocks became low, I went to get some more, but the new stocks were nothing like the pattern I'd been using. Shortly after this something happened, an accident or something like that, on the Mustad production line and they made hooks that were supposed to be 22's but they came out between a 22 and a 20 which became known as 21's. Everybody liked those hooks and within a short space of time everyone was running around buying up supplies of these hooks and when the shops sold out all sorts of deals were being done. But those days are gone now and we are in the era of the laser point and micro barb hooks, but these are not a patch upon the old pattern barbless. Having said all that, we have now got used to the new pattern 90340 and these are what I use most of the time. The main exceptions to this is when chub fishing. If I draw on a shoal of chub I use the Drennan chub hook. These are similar in many respects to the old 90340 but are .001" thicker and they have a micro-barb which I usually squeeze down with a pair of small pliers. The added strength of the wire due to the extra thickness is essential when fishing for chub or when it's a bagging session and they really are a good alternative. I always whip up my hooklengths at home, stoning down the spade to the bare minimum and finishing off the whip with a spot of dope.

There are odd occasions, when things are really hard, that you are looking for very fine presentation. At times like this there is one other pattern I use in size 24's and that is the Kamasan B520's. They are very light and fine and ideal for these sort of situations, but generally it is the other patterns previously mentioned that are used the most.

Dave: To me the hook is the most important part of the tackle I use. I could take you out the back now and show you about 10,000 hooks, of different types, many of which I never use, but I have found over the course of time that I have bought hooks that I didn't like after a short space of time, and then a few years have gone by and suddenly they become the right type for a particular sort of fishing. So I keep them in stock and now I have probably got a greater stock of hooks than the local tackle shop!

I was very much influenced by the likes of Ken, Clive Smith and Max Winters in the 70's and to start with, I was converted to the use of barbless because they used them. As time went by I never experienced any problems of excessive fish loss and I have total faith in them and use them for 90% of my river fishing.

I too remember the era of the 21's and I think my story is worth telling because it does put over some very important points.

During the early days I had about 1,000 size 22's in stock and when these slowly, but surely, ran out I went to buy some more but they just were not available. The pattern had changed and they had disgracefully short points and were no good at all; totally unusable.

Now the Mustad 90340–21. How that came about was as follows: I met up with Jan Porter from Nottingham who had a maggot round at that time supplying the local tackle shops. One day we got talking about hooks and found we both had a preference for the 90340's, and he told me about the 21's, this would be in about 1980. I pestered him for a couple of hundred which he eventually gave me and they really were the business. The problem then was, where could I get some more from. So I went round every tackle shop in the Birmingham area and further afield, trying without success to get some more of these hooks and I used to spend days driving around during the closed season in search of this hook that I wanted; that's how important it was to me. I could get free hooks from anywhere at that time but I wanted and was prepared to pay a good price for this particular pattern. Eventually I went into Austin Clissett's shop in Birmingham, not for hooks as it turned out, but for some pole floats, and while I was there I asked if I could look at the 90340's on the rack, and there were four boxes of 50 of these 21's. Now I kept my mouth shut, but inwardly I was having a minor orgasm over finding these hooks and I asked him if he had any more, and he came down with another 4 large boxes of these, a thousand in each box. I thought, how do you ask discreetly 'How much do you want for these?' because it was April and no one was buying very much tackle and all of a sudden, here was I wanting to buy 4,200 hooks. Anyway the deal was struck and I walked out with a spring in my step despite having written out a cheque that would completely wipe out my bank balance.

I now had plenty in stock, but the problem was that once the news got around everybody wanted some and Ken had a thousand, Dave Howell had a thousand, someone else had a thousand and instead of having enough to last me a lifetime I found when I looked into my stock one day that I was down to my last 150, with the season only half way through. Now when you have got such faith in an item of tackle such as that and all of a sudden it's taken away from you, what do you use as a substitute? I went on record as saying that once these have gone that's it, I'll pack up fishing. That's how bad it was and to be honest it was cracking me up. So I got in touch with Mustad and spoke to the Managing Director, Sid Sowerbutts, and asked him about this particular hook and found that Jan Porter had also been in touch with him. Also I had written articles on the subject of these 21's and everyone was after them. Anyway I sent a letter with hooks sellotaped onto it, explaining that, if they could reproduce them in all the sizes and do it again in a Whisker barb pattern, this would be all the match angler needed. Anyway he sent me two or three hundred samples that were no good and I sent them back saying that I was not after freebies and I was prepared to pay for the right hooks, the outcome of which is, that they have now bought out the 90340's in the odd sizes and the 90342 which is the heavier gauge maggot hook and whilst they are not as good as the original 21's, I can get on with them, have confidence in them and I am a lot happier than I was when I was down to my last 150 originals.

So what I use now are the new pattern 90340's in size 21 and 23's on bottoms up to 1 lb b.s. and the 19's and the heavier gauge 90342's on 1.5 lb b.s. I prefer the heavier 90342's for chub fishing to the Drennan chub hooks that Ken uses, but again its all down to personal preference. There are occasions as well, and I can give you a recent example, where I have been converted to the use of a Whisker barb hook and this was on the Super League semi-final at Medley. I practised on the venue prior to the match and I couldn't believe it. The hook that I have so much confidence in and very rarely lose fish on was completely unsuitable for that venue and I was finding that I was landing only one in 5 fish hooked at that stage and these included roach from 8 to 12 oz each so the use of barbless was quite out of the question. I went through several patterns of hook and on that day I settled for the Drennan Carbon Match which is a Whisker barb pattern with a fairly long point, which again I do not like using. But it just turned out, that on the day, this is what was needed to keep the fish on. The final outcome was that on the match I drew a good peg, hardly lost a fish and won it with 22 lb. If I had stuck with the barbless hook I would probably have weighed in only half as much and been cursing all day at the damage those lost fish were doing to my swim.

Hooks are a very personal thing, but even if you have complete faith in one particular pattern it is still very important to carry around a range of various patterns for those rare situations where one particular hook may not be right on a given day.

Ken: This is just another example of how important it is to keep it simple and to have total confidence in a single item of equipment. So far we have discussed hooks for maggot fishing. For Caster fishing I still use the same pattern, the Mustad 90340 barbless, but I go up to a size 16. I experience no difficulty at all in burying a size 16 barbless in a good quality caster and being barbless, the point comes through the shell on the strike as clean as a whistle. Also of course, a size 16 lends itself well to alternating with a double caster when those odd bonus chub are about and it is plenty strong enough to cope with these fish under normal conditions.

Floats

Q. *What float patterns do you use the most often under match situations? Do you make your own floats or do you consider commercially made floats to be adequate. If you do make your own, what specifications are important in the materials used and in the design?*

Dave: I think that the stick floats available on the market these days are perfect.

Anglers coming into the sport now don't know how fortunate they are with the quality of tackle currently available. In the 70's you had to make your own stick floats to get it right, with heavy bases for long distance casting and light bases for fishing on the drop. But these days, with mass production methods and a full understanding on the part of the manufacturers as to the anglers' requirements, commercially made stick floats cannot be faulted and making your own is just a waste of time.

I use several patterns of stick float to suit the various conditions that I come up against at different times of the year.

In the summer months when fish are feeding at all various levels in the water and many bites can be expected 'on the drop', I prefer to use stick floats made from balsa with light grade cane stems. Unlike the normal stick floats with lignum or heavy cane stems, these tend to lay straighter on the surface, cocking gradually as the shots act upon them. I find this offers less resistance to a taking fish and they are less likely to eject the bait before I can strike and the indication is far more 'positive' (see fig: 2).

These floats are fine when fishing down the side, but the traditional stick floats with lignum stems are essential for casting at longer range across the river. I prefer mine to have standard taper stems, although I know that many northern anglers have taken to using the new pattern floats with bulbous lignum stems.

Another pattern that I do use, particularly under winter conditions when I may need to hold back and slow the bait down, are the wire

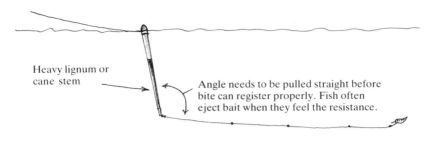

Fig. 2. Fishing with a stick float on the drop.

stem stick floats with the broad shoulder. These are ideal in this situation, the shoulder prevents the float from riding up too high out of the water when held back and they are balanced nicely by the aluminium wire stem, offering very good stability in the water as the float is put through.

The final type of stick floats I use, again in winter conditions when I may wish to bunch the shot as opposed to stringing them out in the traditional manner, is the type made from balsa with the light plastic stems. These perform like a mini all-balsa float and are ideal when the fish are feeding on or near the bottom. As I have mentioned, I will bunch the shot together about 3 ft from the hook and just have a couple of small droppers below. These work great when the surface is a bit boily due to extra water in the river.

Ken: I've got to agree with him. I used to make my own stick floats. Clive Smith and I would go through the most painstaking hours to get them right and for every 6 we made, we would end up throwing 4 away because they were not quite right. We didn't know why but we knew they would not work properly. Now you can go into a shop, select the size you want, line it up and check that it's true, it's painted beautifully and is spot on for weight etc. There is no way that an individual can compete and make floats as good as those you can buy now.

Dave: When we come onto wagglers then that is a different kettle of fish altogether. Most companies make a reasonable straight waggler, but having said that I still prefer to make my own, because it is cheaper and I can use different thicknesses over the various lengths etc. But when it come to insert wagglers, no company, in my opinion makes a decent insert waggler to compare to my own. In most cases they make the insert too short, or they use a different material for the insert to the peacock inserts that I find essential. This is mainly due to the difficulty of working with thinner pieces of peacock quill on a mass production basis. Most commercial wagglers are made by using cane inserts and this is far too sensitive when you are dragging a couple of feet of line along the bed of a river. You need the buoyancy of peacock to cope with this and prevent 'false' bites. The very fine inserts only make this problem even worse, added to the fact that at long range you cannot see them. These are all right for still water fishing but for river fishing you must have either straight peacock or peacock floats with peacock inserts. There are one or two companies now who are getting it half right for inserted floats, but for my part I still prefer to make my own wagglers.

Q. *What balance do you look for with regards to the length of insert?*

Dave: It depends upon the venue really. If I am fishing a small hook I use the lightest float that I can to get to the distance I want to fish. On the Warwickshire Avon and parts of the Trent this would be 2 AA to 2½ AA capacity, and the insert would need to be sensitive to about 3 no. 8 shot fitted down the line, so it is important that the locking shot sink the float down to the insert, so I can see these shots acting upon it as they fall through the water. Then I would be looking towards an insert that was about 2″ long. On deeper water or slower water such as on the Middle Trent, I would have a lot more lead down the line, so to read the drop on this I would have an insert up to 4″ long. But generally I work on the principle of, the longer or bigger the float the longer the insert will be.

Ken: Of all the materials that have been tried over the years, personally speaking, I can find nothing to beat peacock quill. A number of substitutes have been tried from plastic drinking straws to various types of reed, but nothing else is as light and as buoyant as peacock quill. It's robust, you can work with the different diameters and the most important quality is, that because it is so light, you end up casting the weight under the float and not the float itself. This is very important and it is the key to complete control.

The only other material which goes with peacock quill on those occasions that you need to have a body on it to increase its shot carrying capacity, is polystyrene. Many of the commercial floats use balsa for bodies, but in my opinion this is too heavy and upsets the balance of the float.

Another thing that upsets the balance and is totally unsuitable for floats used in running water, is internal loading. This totally destroys the natural buoyancy of the float and whenever you mend the line to a loaded float it takes much longer to reappear on the surface than a float which is unloaded and is trimmed with just shots on the line. I don't know why this is, I doubt if there is a proper scientific explanation, but it is a fact. An unloaded float comes up quicker and is less affected by surface boils or the resistance of your hooklength being dragged along the river bed. You can walk it through the swim much better than a float which is loaded.

But having said that, if you are fishing a very slow moving river such as the Nene or the Welland, where there is a strong wind, then you need the float to be loaded, because when you cast, it goes into the water like an arrow, completely burying itself and helps you to sink your line without it being pulled away from the far shelf and of course due to its sensitivity, it helps you to see the bites on the drop. These are the occasions when loading and cane inserts are an advantage. But for fishing faster flowing rivers they are a handicap and only unloaded peacock floats work properly in these conditions.

The 1989/1990 Superteam

Ken Giles displays some of his impressive array of trophies. The fruits of a long and successful career.

Dave Harrell with a superb catch of Avon chub.
(Photograph courtesy of Angling Times)

Ken Giles in action using a Topper at Twyfords Farm on the Warwickshire Avon.

Dave Harrell with a net of quality Avon roach.
(Photograph courtesy of Angling Times)

Dave Harrell playing the last fish of the day on the Warwickshire Avon.
(Photograph courtesy of Angling Times)

Dave Harrell fishing the Avon. Note efficient tackle layout.

Dave Harrell unhooking a quality Avon chub.
(Photograph courtesy of Angling Times)

A sample of the continental groundbaits now very much in favour.

Fishing the Stick Float

Q. *When you reach your peg on a river, how do you go about assessing its potential and what equipment would you set up initially?*

Dave: I think the important thing is to find out beforehand exactly where you are going and collect as much information as you can about the venue, particularly if it is a water you are not familiar with. I often hear it said that because of the situation we are in, at the forefront of the match fishing fraternity, we've got it easy. Well we haven't really. Over the course of time we have to talk to many people and find out from local tackle shops and friends who are familiar with the venue as to its nature; is it fast flowing or slow flowing, in spate or normal level? What species are predominant, is it roach, dace or chub and also what sort of weights are currently winning matches? You might be looking at 5 lb or 6 lb, or you may be looking at 30 lb. Your planning before a match is essential and will dictate how much bait you are going to take and also what tackle will be needed.

That part assessed, you then need to have some idea after you have drawn your peg as to whether you have drawn a favourable area or are going to struggle. If it is an Open Match, there will normally be a high percentage of local anglers present and they are normally pretty forthcoming with this information, particularly if you have drawn badly. You do of course sometimes get what we call 'bum info', but on the whole you will usually get an honest opinion.

Ken: I agree with Dave on this. If we classify ourselves as sportsmen, angling is the same as any other sport in this respect, be it golf, tennis, football etc. They would not just turn up at an event and go in blind, they will have had practice and discussion of some sort. Take for example golf. A top golfer, before a tournament, will walk the course with his Caddy, taking note of its geography, length and position of holes, direction of prevailing winds, condition of green surfaces etc, so that on the day, he will know exactly what he is doing. His experience will enable

Fig. 13. Efficient tackle layout for fishing in the standing position.

him to assess what changes he may have to make to his base plan to enable him to cope with any sudden changes in weather conditions such as strong winds and rain etc. You cannot just turn up at strange venues and expect to catch a lot of fish if you haven't done your homework. Your homework can be done in a number of ways. You can stay in and pick up the phone, asking around people you know who are familiar with the current form of the venue, or you can go and have a look at the water and chat with the locals on the bank and visit the local tackle shop which is always the centre of current information of form, methods and baits.

Once this homework has been done and you eventually get to your peg, you have a good idea what species you are after and what methods need to be employed to catch them. You can set up your tackle and your experience will tell you if it's going to be purely a stick float day, a waggler day, or if you will be using a combination of both. Once you have established the geography of the swim, you have the confidence to get on with the job, using the right method and approach.

Dave: One of the most important and beneficial changes that has happened in recent times, is being allowed to plumb your depth prior to the start of a match. It is a recent thing that has only been allowed in

my area in the last couple of seasons, but for myself it's a godsend. I
normally put a stick float on the line, any size will do, say 5 No. 4's
if the peg looks about 6 or 7 ft deep, put on a plummet and start plumbing
around. You may be shocked to find you've got as much as 12 ft of
water or you may only have as little as 3 ft. I will assess the general
depth of the swim and then plumb around different parts of the swim
at say, one rod length out, two rod lengths out and so on and if the
river is not too wide, I will also make a couple of casts over to the far
side to see if there is any variation establishing the complete geography
of the swim, noting the position of any shelves, ledges and gulleys etc.

It is very difficult to generalise upon float sizes, but as a rough guide,
if you have got 5 or 6 ft of water in front of you then you would be
looking to starting with a 5 No. 4 float. If you find you have 10 or 12 ft,
this would be stepped up to a 7 or 8 No. 4 stick float. If conditions
are far from ideal due to a stiff upstream breeze or a bit of extra water
pushing through, then it may be necessary to go heavier than this, but
once you get up to 4 B.B. and find you have to go heavier still, then
I would consider using an all-balsa float, as stick floats bigger than 4
B.B. tend to be unwieldy and do not perform properly.

Ken: Dave has covered everything there and I have nothing to add other
than what I would use in conditions dictating the use of heavier floats.
Again this comes down to personal preference, but in these circumstances
I would use a Topper. This is a large crow quill with a balsa or Elder
Pith body also known as an Avon float. They are usually used with No.
4's or B.B.'s bunched about 3 ft from the hook with one or two smaller
droppers. Personally I prefer to use a tungsten olivette in place of the
bunched shot. (See fig. 24).

Q.   *What would be your starting shotting patterns when using a stick
float and what type of shot do you use down the line, i.e. bunches of small
No. 8's or larger sizes of non-toxic shots?*

Dave: Obviously the lead shot ban that came into force a couple of
years ago has created problems with the use of No. 6's and No. 4's.
Nowadays I tend to favour the use of bunches of smaller shots. Invariably,
if the water is of a steady sort of pace, then I would use a Number
10 shot on the hooklength to start with. This would be placed initially
about 10″ from the hook on an 18″ hook length, with number 8's spread
out above this to make up the total shotting capacity. The first couple
of No. 8's would be singles, 4″ or 5″ apart and the rest would be bunched
equally in two's or three's, again 4″ or 5″ apart. (See Fig. 14). This will
allow for an endless number of variations in bait presentation to be carried
out during the course of the match and by moving the shots about, I

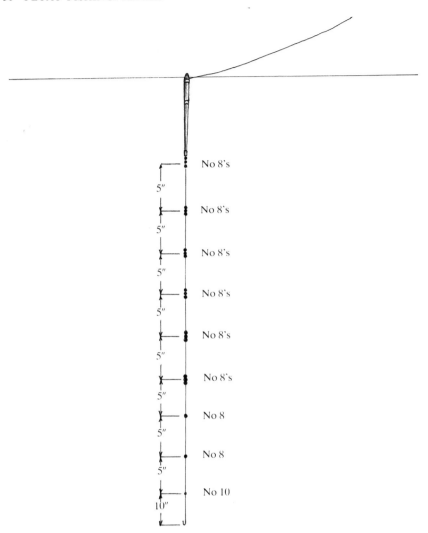

Fig. 14. Basic stick float shotting pattern using bunches of No. 8 shot.

can alter the speed at which the bait falls through the water for taking fish either on a slow drop, or, by moving the bunches downwards, get the bait down quickly when the fish are feeding on the bottom. (See Fig. 15).

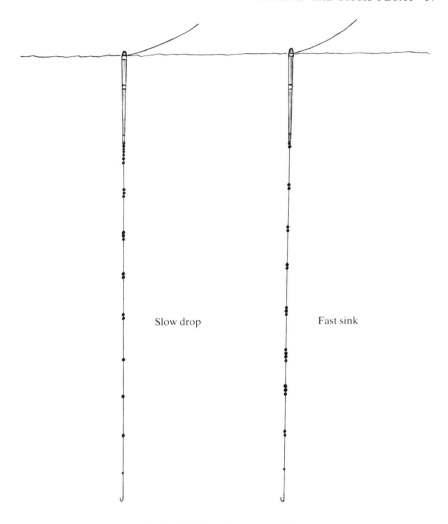

Fig. 15. Stick float shotting variations.

Ken: I use basically the same set up, but over the last 12 months or so I have been using only 10″ hook lengths instead of my previous 18″ ones. This is something that has come about due to my increasing use of the pole and that I have now adopted for fishing with the running line. The big advantage is that if I break off or need to change my hook size I can do so without having to waste time re-shotting the hooklength. All my shot is on my main line with my indicating shot just above where it joins the hooklength. I have found that this does not interfere at all with the presentation of the bait and during the course of a match where I may have to make a number of hook changes or am losing hooks due to snags in the swim, the time saving is considerable and time is always the match angler's greatest enemy.

Dave: Talking about time saving, I think it's very useful to carry stick floats around on winders, complete with hook and shotting. I don't make them up at home, but at the end of the day's fishing; the tackle I have made up at the bankside is wound on to the winder plus 4 or 5 ft of line above the float. This is very useful on those occasions when you, say, pull out of a fish whilst playing it and the tackle flies back and tangles, or, if you have drawn a long walk and do not have enough time when you reach your peg to make up a new tackle from scratch. All you have to do is tie the loop to your main line using either a blood knot or a grinner knot and unwind the tackle. Re-set the depth and you are away again in the minimum of time.

Ken: Yes, I have also started to do this and its very comforting to know that you have this facility. It can only add to your confidence as well as saving you time. It also allows you to keep your feeding and fishing rhythm uninterrupted so if you have fish in front of you when an accident happens you do not risk losing them due to your feeding rhythm being interrupted, as often used to happen. This is now especially important with the current use of bunches of small shots as opposed to single larger ones. It can take 5 or 10 minutes to re-tackle a stick float rig and anything can happen to your swim in that time. Even if you stop between putting on each shot to feed the swim, it means you will take even longer to re-tackle and when you finally start fishing again, another 10 or 15 minutes will be lost trying to get back into your fishing rhythm.

The use of winders is of course another of those ideas which have been borrowed from the continent and although the use of these bunches of small shot was initially forced upon us, it has now turned to our advantage, as we now find that due to this finess, we are able to present our tackle more effectively than ever before and with less resistance to the shots in the water, making for far more positive bite indication.

Dave: It is also very important to keep track of your depth changes, noting, by using your rod rings as an indicator, your original depth so you can assess your current depth at any given time. Then, if you need to put on a fresh tackle you can immediately set it to the appropriate depth and be instantly back in touch with the fish. I am fortunate in having a good memory when noting these positions, but some people find it helpful to carry a bottle of typewriter correction fluid with them and to use this to mark their depth positions on the rod blank. This also comes in handy if you have to change your hook length or, for example, if you lose touch with the fish during the course of the match. By having this depth marker you know you can always return to your original depth and work again from there. Often during the course of a match, I may move my float 2 or 3 ft away from this starting position and it's always comforting to know I can return to it as and when I need to.

Q. *Many anglers have fixed ideas on fishing the stick float. Some always hold back and put the tackle through slower than the flow. Others insist upon allowing the tackle to run through at the speed of the current. Top anglers such as yourselves know instinctively how to put the float through correctly and when to vary the speed. What signs do you look for and how do you control the tackle in response? What changes do you make to the shotting patterns to achieve this?*

Ken: Holding back is only one of many methods used in the stick float angler's repertoire and is generally only used after the first frost of winter or in similar conditions when the fish are semi-torpid and are not moving around in the water chasing the bait.

On these occasions they will only take a bait that is literally put into their mouths. They instinctively know that they have got to feed but not at the expense of losing energy in the process. This means that you will be looking at inching the bait through, on or near to the bottom, as it is here that the fish normally lie under these conditions. There are of course some occasions during the summer months when this sort of situation also occurs and by holding back now and again the odd bonus fish can be tempted in this way. But generally at this time of year, fish are all over the river, at all different levels in the water and holding back would be the exception rather than the rule.

Another way of assessing when to hold back is by the nature of the river you are actually fishing. The Trent tends to be a river where you run it at them, in other words it's seldom that you need to hold back. This may be due to its comparatively higher winter water temperatures caused by the influx of warm water from the many power stations lining its banks. In the Midlands, the Avon, the Severn and venues similar to these, tend to be the venues where you often need to hold back, not all the time, but you do tend to hold back more than on the Trent, although I must re-emphasise that this tends to be after the first frost.

On those occasions that you do have to do it there are several ways of achieving it. If you have an upstream wind situation, then by keeping your rod held high and allowing the breeze to take hold of the line, the wind can do it for you. Another method is to use rod tip control. You move the rod upstream, allowing plenty of line to come off the spool of the reel, then follow the float downstream with the rod tip, putting the tackle through at the required speed, which is usually half to two thirds of the speed of the flow. It pays to vary the speed until you get the required response. The other method is to smoothly feed the line directly off the spool at the required rate. (See Fig. 16). This needs a lot of practice before you get the right feel and can put the tackle through smoothly without jerking it. Which method you use is a personal thing. You need to practice and use whichever method you find the most comfortable and efficient. In the old days of the centrepin reel, the natural resistance caused by the drag of the reel would do this job for you, but with the fixed spool and closed face reels, the methods I have described are the ones to use.

The most important point that must be covered on stick float fishing is the need to keep the line behind the float at all times. This is a must. It just does not work if the line is allowed to go in front of the float. This rule applies whether you are holding back or running through. You are constantly working to keep this bow from forming and during the course of trotting your float down a twelve yard swim you may have to mend the line and bring it back behind the float 4 or 5 times. This must be done as smoothly as possible without pulling the tackle off line.

To achieve this, you must treat your line with silicon spray and the last 4 or 5 feet of line immediately behind the float must be coated with Mucilin or Vaseline. This is one of the important 'little' things that make such a big difference. By doing this, you can lift your line off of the water much more easily, without disturbing the tackle and pulling it off line. The float will then go down the swim perfectly and you will be walking the bait straight into the fish's mouth.

A good floating line is essential. Any line which has a tendency to sink is useless for this type of fishing. Every time you try to mend the line, as it is lifted out of the water the tackle will be dragged out of position. This is another reason why it is important to replace your line after every 5 or 6 outings. As a line gets older, it has a greater tendency to sink, so by always having fresh line on your reels this problem is easily overcome.

So far we have talked about the importance of putting the tackle through smoothly, whether holding back or running through. But there are times when you are dace fishing, or sometimes when fishing for chub, when you do not want it going through smoothly. On these occasions it pays to trap the line on the spool, causing the tackle to check and the float to lift up in the water, which in turn causes the tail and the bait to rise up anything from a few inches to a few feet in strong flows,

Fig. 16. Feeding the line from the spool whilst trotting.

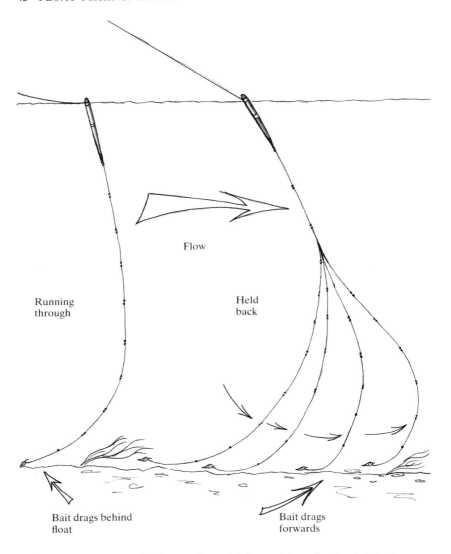

Flow

Running
through

Held
back

Bait drags behind
float

Bait drags
forwards

Fig. 17. Dave Harrell's theory of how stick float tackle works when held back.

then letting it go again, allowing the tail to fall. This can be repeated
4 or 5 times during the course of the swim and often as the tackle is
released the float goes under and you have a fish.

This is just another technique incorporated into the repertoire of stick float fishing, to be tried when bites are not forthcoming by using more conventional methods. I cannot explain exactly when to use it, or when I actually use it. I just sometimes get a gut feeling, especially on a cold, hard day, that a chub may be there in the swim and not taking a bait put through in the normal way, but by doing it, I induce the fish to have a go.

Dave: I agree with everything Ken has said. At the start of a match, particularly in the winter months when I use a stick float more than I do in the summer, as in the West Midlands area a stick float is essentially a winter method, due to the higher water levels and the need, on occasions, to slow the bait down, I always start by running the float through at the speed of the current. This usually gives me a guide to the overall depth of the swim throughout its length. Although I have plumbed the depth at the beginning of the match, I do need to know at what depth I can put the float through at, without getting false bites or snagging etc.

If possible I always start off by having as much depth on as possible, dragging the bottom by as much as two feet if the swim will allow it. I juggle around with the bottom shots to try to achieve this. Obviously, if there is a particularly bad snag in the peg and I am constantly getting caught up on it, then I try to find a snag free run either closer in or further out, but failing this I then have to shorten off until I can clear it. But assuming that I have got a nice clean river bed to go at, then I will always start off by running the float through at the pace of the current, adding depth accordingly. I would keep on doing this for the first 15 to 20 minutes, then if there was no response I would try shortening off and coming up in the water. When I do hold back, I do not hold back really hard. I think this is a misconception, heightened by articles and illustrations in the angling press. There are a lot of rubbish diagrams done about the way stick floats and the bait go down a swim and I think it's important to try to dispel them.

If, as we are led to believe, the bait always goes down the swim ahead of the float, then you would have to hold back really hard all the way down the swim to achieve this. I believe that, in fact, the reverse is true and that due to the fact that the speed of the current near the river bed is a lot slower than at the surface, the bait drags along behind the float, similar to how it does with a waggler. When the float is held back or checked, the bait is dragged forwards along the bottom (see Fig. 17). I'm not completely certain, because we cannot prove it unless someone is prepared to go down with an underwater camera, but this is what I think happens and the important thing is of course, that it works. To us that is all that really matters, we don't really need to know how it works, we just need to know that it does.

I think that the only time that the bait is in front of the float, as shown in the traditional diagrams, is when the tackle is falling through the water immediately after casting, and whilst the angler is holding it back to straighten it out. But during the actual trotting process I am pretty certain that the hook length is travelling behind the float. One other thing that I think is important to point out is that whilst many anglers realise and accept the importance of fishing well off the bottom with wagglers, they do not realise the importance of doing the same with stick floats. For some reason, many of them plumb the depth and then tend to fish either over depth or just tripping the bottom and they do miss out on a lot of fish. I remember on numerous occasions when I have caught a lot of roach, fishing 2 ft deep in 8 or 10 ft of water and I have been unable to buy a bite whilst fishing on or near the bottom. This only amplifies the need to keep changing your depth and shotting constantly until you determine where the fish are feeding. So the important thing is, that regardless of the method, be it stick float or waggler, you must keep changing your depth around between being a couple of feet over depth to a couple of feet below the surface. Also, it is important to keep altering your shotting to find and to keep in touch with the fish, although having said that, I do not change my basic shotting pattern that much. Most of the changes I make are to the bottom two or three shot, leaving the rest of the rig more or less the same. Sometimes, I will move the bunches of shot closer to the float, giving me a much slower fall when the fish are taking on the drop. If the fish are feeding on or near the bottom, or there is a bit of extra water pushing through, I will sometimes bunch them down towards the lower half. But generally, it is the last two or three single shots that I will move about the most. Again the key to success is to keep things relatively simple and not get too complicated. This can only serve to confuse you.

During a five hour match, which is a long time, although at the time it may not seem it, you must give yourself time to allow ten minutes or so on a certain shotting pattern or a certain depth before you change it and try something different. Changes do not always bring an instant response. But if you can get yourself a 20 minute or half hour catching spell on one particular shotting pattern or depth then that could win you that match. I am continually being asked 'What are your secrets?' Well there are no secrets. It's all down to confidence, hard work, common sense and varying my approach until I find the fish and the best way that they want the bait presented on the day.

Fishing the Waggler

Let us now discuss waggler fishing.

Q. *Whilst I have always achieved a reasonable degree of success fishing rivers at close range, I have always struggled when fishing the waggler at any sort of distance and this is a problem shared by many anglers. What are the important points to consider when fishing the waggler at long range, i.e. should you cast upstream, downstream or straight in front? Should you sink the line or leave it on the surface? Should you mind the line or leave it to bow? How do you cope with strong downstream winds?*

Ken: You should always cast downstream. If the water is moving from left to right under good conditions, you would cast to what we call the one o'clock position. 12 o'clock is straight in front of you, so you would cast slightly downstream to the one o'clock position (see Fig. 18). You gain nothing from casting upstream or in front of yourself. The golden rule is that the stronger the wind the further down the swim you cast. The one o'clock position is the normal position in light winds, but in really strong winds you may have to cast much further downstream in an effort to eliminate the bow which will inevitably form in your line if you cast upstream or in front of you (see Fig. 19).

When you cast a waggler you normally use an overhead cast and it is important to have enough weight on the line to reach where you want to fish comfortably. If you need to force the cast your float is not big enough and you must change it. Don't be frightened to use plenty of weight when waggler fishing. We spoke earlier of using the ideal float making material which is peacock quill. This is where it comes into its own, because all you are having to do is to cast the lead and the float follows it. You do not have the situation that you get with other floats, where the lead is pulling one way and the float is pulling another. You can concentrate on just one thing, having enough weight to get where you want to and putting it into the exact spot. So, you do not select the float you want, you select the amount of weight you want to reach where you intend to fish and then pick a float to suit that. If you are

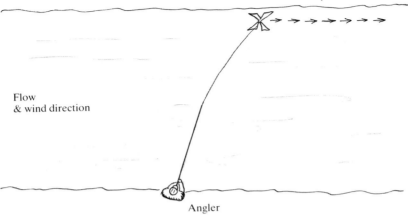

"1 o'clock" position correct

Flow
& wind direction

Angler

Fig. 18. Casting position of waggler under good conditions.

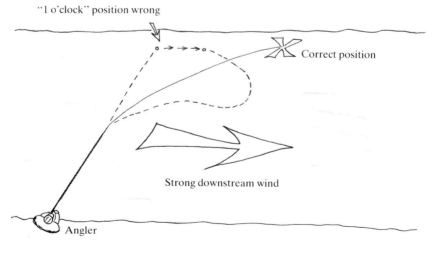

"1 o'clock" position wrong

Correct position

Strong downstream wind

Angler

Fig. 19. Casting position in extreme downstream winds. If casts were made to 1 o'clock, the line will soon bow out of control, pulling the tackle out of line.

fishing in deeper water, or fast flowing water where you want a bit more weight than usual down the line to get down to the fish, then you will select a float that is that much bigger, which will give you that additional amount of weight.

You ask whether you sink the line or leave it on the surface? This is dependent upon the strength of the wind. Ideally, you want to leave the line on the surface. You can see where it is and how much bow is forming and it is much easier to lift it through the air on the strike than it is through the water. Also, providing the wind is not too strong, you can with practice mend the line to the float without pulling it under and this is the ideal situation. Unfortunately these ideal situations do not always arise and in conditions of really fierce downstream winds, you must not be frightened to sink the line. In these conditions you may need to put on twice the normal weight to allow you to keep in control of the tackle and to 'feel' the float down the swim. By this I mean that every few yards or so down the swim you must trap the line coming off of the spool and move the rod tip slightly upstream, pulling the bow out of the line. When the bow is taken up you should 'feel' the float and you may see it dip slightly in the water. This means your line is nice and tight again to the float and you can carry on with the trot, knowing that you have ideal bait presentation and the float is not being dragged through the swim, by the bow, faster than the speed of the current.

Dave: Yes I go along with most of what Ken has said. You can get a situation when there is a bad downstream wind and where the water in front of the line you are fishing is running through at a much faster pace, especially if you are trotting the far bank. How you cope with this depends upon the length of your peg.

In tight pegging situations where you only have 12 yards instead of 15 or 20, it can pay you to keep feeding the line off of the spool at a rate that allows the bow to form without it affecting the speed of the float, or pulling it away from your line of trot. When the float goes under you must then sweep the bow up off of the surface to connect with the fish, and often this means the rod tip will be way past the back of your head in the field behind and you will need to reel in several yards of line before the size of the fish is felt.

Where you have a reasonable length of swim to go at then it is as Ken has said, you must put on extra weight and sink the line. This means where you would normally be using a float of 2 A.A.A. you will instead use a 2 swan float or even heavier on occasions, to keep control. Instead of casting to the one o'clock position, you will have to cast almost half way down the swim. This may mean that once the bait has settled you may only be able to fish effectively over 4 or 5 yards of the swim, so you must try to concentrate your feed and presentation to take fish

Ken with a haul of 40 pounds plus of bream using waggler tacics near Rotterdam, Holland.

Ken during a match practice catching bream on the waggler.

from this small area. Often you will find that you can do this and get regular bites from this area, whereas if you try to fish the full length of the swim in these conditions you will end up getting no bites at all.

It is also important, as Ken has already said, to keep in touch with the float. The worst thing in the world is to have a big bow 'under' the surface. There is no way that you can pick this up against the resistance of the water and if it is allowed to form it will start to drag the tackle through at an unnatural rate. This is why you need to cast so far down the swim in these conditions, to give yourself a few yards head start before the bow can form and due to the narrower angle, you can keep your line tighter to the float over a longer period (see Fig. 19).

Q. *With reference to locking shots. We have mentioned using 2 A.A.A. floats and also the need on occasions to use 2 swan shots. Do you actually use 2 A.A.A. or 2 swan shots to lock the floats, or do you use bunches of smaller shots?*

Dave: I very rarely use swan shots unless I am going to use really big floats such as the ones I have mentioned that I use in Ireland. Then I would use swan shots. But for float fishing in this country I would normally break these down into groups of A.A.A.s or B.B.s. How I normally shot up a waggler is as follows: I use an A.A.A. each side of the float, and if it were a 2 swan float I would use 3 A.A.A.s and a B.B., splitting the rest of the shot needed into bunches of No. 8's (see Fig. 22).

I may find that I am catching with 3 No. 8's down the line, with the others under the bulk shot and then later on I may need to bring these down and fish with 6 or 7 No. 8's spread down the line. So I always ensure that some of the shot is split into these smaller sizes to allow me to vary the presentation during the course of the match (see Fig. 21). The main consideration when deciding how much shot to use down the line, is the depth and flow of the swim and the time of the year. In the summer months in a swim of say 6 ft in depth, I would be looking to taking fish at any depth in the water. So, I would use an inserted float with only 2 or 3 No. 8's or 10's spread down the line. The bulk shot will sink the float down to the insert and I will be counting the fall of the small shots through the water as they act on the setting of the insert. After a couple of trots down I know exactly when these shots will fall and any interruption or delay in this pattern will be due to fish taking the bait on the drop and naturally I shall strike. Should I find that I am constantly getting bites at say 4 ft, then I will shallow off to get a more positive registration (see Fig. 22). In the winter months when the fish tend to feed on or near the bottom I will want to get down to the fish more quickly, so I will bring more shots down the line

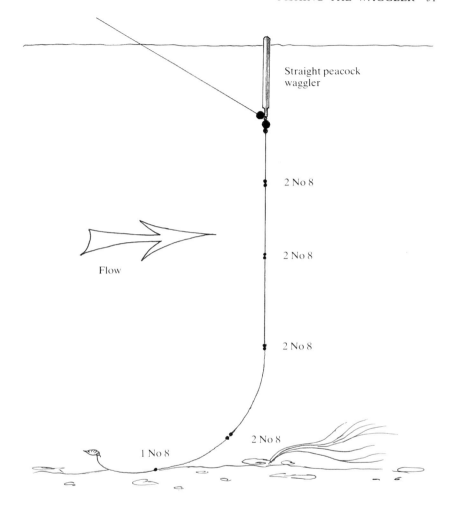

Fig. 20. Basic waggler rig—for dragging overdepth. Shot positions variable.

to achieve this and cut down upon the time it takes to get the bait down to the fish. But I will still be looking for drop bites in the lower third of the water as the fish rise up in response to my loose feed. In deeper water of 10 or 12 ft I may incorporate quite heavy bulk shot at two thirds depth, that is a third up from the bottom, to get the bait down to the fish in the shortest possible time and then read off for drop bites with

Fig. 21. Shotting a waggler. Note the spare No. 8 droppers.

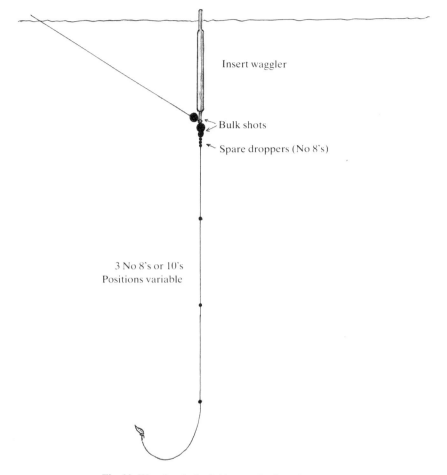

Insert waggler

Bulk shots

Spare droppers (No 8's)

3 No 8's or 10's
Positions variable

Fig. 22. Waggler rig for fishing on the drop (summer).

the last couple of shots (see Fig. 23).

Ken: Yes, my approach is exactly the same but I would like to emphasise one point: it is very important to have the potential to vary your presentation, as Dave has said. By using small bunches of No. 8's there is no end to the variations you can make and it is more important with a waggler than with the stick float to utilise them as much as possible. We will be talking about feeding methods more fully later on, but it is essential to get your hook bait falling through the water and reaching the point in the swim at which the fish are feeding, at the same time and in the same way as your loose feed. This will vary during the course of a match, so it is important that if you should lose touch with the fish that you vary your depth and shotting until you find them again.

Q. *How do you decide whether to use an insert or a straight waggler? Are there occasions when sensitivity can be a handicap?*

Dave: An insert is essential for detecting bites on the drop and whenever I expect to catch fish at various levels in the water, my first choice is to use an insert waggler. When the fish are not moving around the water quite so freely and you need to slow the rig down, this is normally achieved by fishing several feet over depth with the bait and the bottom shot dragging along the bottom. Under these circumstances you would use a straight peacock (see Fig. 23).

You may on occasions need to have as much as an inch of float tip showing above the surface to allow for the drag of the tackle and to prevent the occurrence of 'false bites'. A fine insert in these circumstances would be a handicap, especially on faster flowing venues. As the tackle goes through the swim, the float tip will rise and fall as the tackle is dragged along and then released by the variations of the river bed. Under these circumstances it may take a lot of adjustments to get everything working properly, but once this has been achieved and you have got used to reading the rhythm of the float through that particular swim, bites will be positive and unmistakable.

Ken: The other important consideration is range and visibility, especially in very choppy conditions. We have mentioned the occasions when you need to sink the line and 'feel' the tackle. This can only be done by using a straight waggler. An insert in these conditions would be a handicap, as you would be continually striking at false indications. When you tighten up to straighten the bow, you must have the buoyancy of a thick tip to pull against, otherwise the method will just not work. Again, only practice and experience can teach you this.

Q. *When fishing small and medium width rivers where the far bank is in comfortable casting range, the natural features such as shelves and ledges and overhanging trees are obvious fishing lines. How do you decide which line to fish on broad, featureless rivers such as the Trent or Severn?*

Dave: Obviously, with the river Trent when you get down around the Nottingham area and on parts of the Severn, fishing the far bank is impossible.

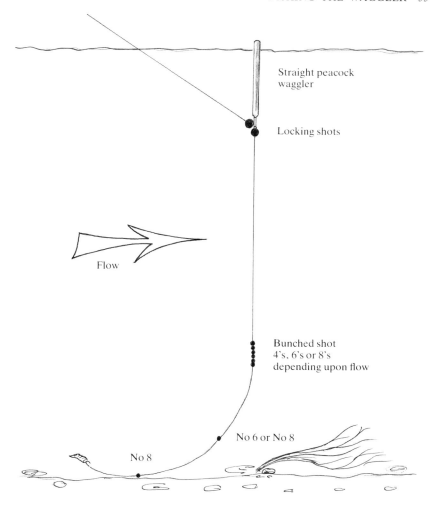

Straight peacock waggler

Locking shots

Flow

Bunched shot
4's, 6's or 8's
depending upon flow

No 6 or No 8

No 8

Fig. 23. Winter waggler rig for fast sink. Can be fished overdepth or just off the bottom.

The important thing is not to overstretch yourselves. Wind plays an important part in deciding your approach and you must fish to within your feeding capability which is also governed by the strength and the direction of the wind. I see many anglers start off by feeding and fishing at the limit the conditions will allow at the beginning of a match and as the wind picks up during the course of the day they are unable to continue on that line. You need to assess what conditions are likely to be later on in the match and ensure that you can adjust accordingly. It is no good fishing a line and then finding you cannot get your feed out to it later on.

What I tend to do if there is a bit of a breeze blowing, is to feed two waggler lines, with a view to coming back onto the inside line if the wind gets too strong and I am unable to get my feed out to the far line. So you may have a situation where I feed and fish a line at 5 or 6 rods out and also lightly feed a line at about 3 rods out. Then, if the wind gets up and I can no longer fish the far line, I still have a swim which has been built up, to use as a reserve and hopefully bring the fish in as well from the outside line.

I also feel that it pays to feed two lines like this anyway, to allow you to rest one against the other. You may have an hour of catching fish out on the far line and then it can pay you to rest it for a while whilst you pinch a few pounds of fish from the near line and alternate between the two during the course of the match. The important thing of course is to keep both lines constantly fed. This will build up the confidence of the fish in each line to feed and you can keep the catch rate going without completely depleting one area of fish. I feel that it is important to still keep some fish in the swim because the vibrations they send out whilst moving around feeding attract others. It is always much harder to attract other fish into a swim which has been fished out.

Ken: I have to agree. So often on these venues when you get to your peg, the weather is quite reasonable. Then, just as you are getting a few fish together, the wind gets up and makes it impossible to continue on that line, and unless you have fed a reserve line it can cost you half the match building up another part of the swim. It is important for any person who intends to take match fishing seriously, to learn to understand the weather charts shown on the weather reports and understand the weather patterns which affect this country. The prevailing wind is usually south west to westerly, which means that on a majority of the rivers in this country such as the Trent, the Nene, the Welland and the Thames, you are going to get the wind blowing down stream or in the case of the east bank of the Severn, in your face. Wind speeds tend to die down around dawn and then pick up again during the course of the day so you can have the first hour of a match in near perfect conditions and then be faced with a howling downstreamer during the next four hours. By analysing the weather charts and noting how close together the isobars are, you can anticipate the conditions and base your match plan accordingly. If there is a big ridge of high pressure over the country, you know that the winds will be light and you have complete control of the situation. If you know that a front will be coming across the country during the day, you realise that conditions are going to change, so you concentrate on getting the maximum from the swim whilst conditions will still allow it and build up a reserve line for when the conditions alter.

Dave: If I know it is going to be a waggler day I will set up a couple of rods with two different rigs. A heavy rig with plenty of weight down the line if the water is quite deep, and a lighter rig with just a few dust shots down the line, for fishing in mid water and on the drop. This gives me more versatility to keep experimenting with my depth and feeding ratio, which, just as when stick float fishing, is very important. In fact I would go as far as to say, that when waggler fishing I am ringing the changes far more often than I need to do with the stick float. The amount of times that chub, and as has been found in recent years, also roach, feed off the bottom, particularly during the summer months is quite amazing and because years ago anglers had it drummed into them that roach were mainly bottom feeders, many club level anglers are far too preoccupied with fishing on or near the bottom all of the time. I am sure if they made a deliberate effort to start coming up to half depth or even shallower on occasions when they are not catching, they would be in for a very pleasant surprise and have a better understanding of fishes feeding habits and appreciate the pounds of fish they have missed catching over the years by being too slavish to what can only be described as 'old wives tales'.

Ken: Yes there are many myths going around in angling be it to do with fish, baits or tackle, and hopefully we will have dispelled quite a few in this book. Anglers are always keen to learn new information, but you must never take anything as gospel, no matter from how authoritative the source may seem to be. The top match anglers only get there and stay there by hard work; thinking things out for themselves and by adapting and improving upon established methods and techniques. The important thing to them is to keep it simple, but effective. When you really analyse the techniques of fishing with a waggler nothing could be more straightforward or simple. You simply attach a piece of peacock quill to the line by the bottom end only. Shot it up with about 75% of the weight around the float, cast it in and allow it to go through the swim completely unhindered. Move your smaller shots up or down to speed up or slow down the baits fall through the water and keep changing your depth until you find the fish. Now what is complicated about that? You do not need to know any complicated physics formulae, or how to mix any chemical potions. You do not need to be a super fit athlete or have an I.Q. of 150+. What you do need is an open, thinking mind, a determination to succeed and lots of practice and experience to give you the confidence. Hopefully the information provided in the book will help you to put it all together and to see a significant improvement in your results.

Other Methods

Q. *We have discussed the use of stick floats and wagglers on rivers. What other patterns do you carry for river fishing and under what circumstances would they be used? What would be the basic shotting patterns and what adjustments would you make?*

Ken: The only other pattern that I carry around with me is a 'Topper Haskins'. This is a crow quill with an Elder Pith or balsa body and is fished top and bottom like a stick float. Some people know them better as Avon floats, but these can be also made of balsa and cane, which are materials that I do not use. So I will refer to it as the Topper, as that is only made from balsa or Pith on crow quill. They are very useful in the winter months when you draw a swim with a lot of depth, or one which has a lot of boils and swirls on the surface close in. They were initially designed for use on the Bristol Avon and are normally used with B.B.s or No. 4's bunched together in a string with one or two droppers below. I prefer to use one of the new Tungsten Olivettes, which are smaller and neater, and lock this onto the line with a locking shot either side (see Fig. 24). It is small and compact and you can cast it anywhere without getting tangles. The olivette takes the bait straight down to the fish, which under these conditions nearly always tend to be on or near the bottom and you can catch any species with it. Roach, chub, barbel, anything and the surprising thing is you can often switch from a heavy stick float to a topper after a blank period and suddenly find the swim is alive with fish that would just not respond to the presentation of a bait on a stick float. Due to the fact that you are taking fish from around the bottom on this method, you would not make many adjustments to the shotting or depth other than to the drop shot. These you would experiment with if bites were not forthcoming, but basically the rig as drawn in Fig. 24 is as it would be used.

There is one very important point that I must make about using this rig. You cannot fish it effectively unless you use either a closed face reel or a fixed spool reel with an automatic dab bail arm. Due to the nature of the rig, with the float bouncing around well up the rod and

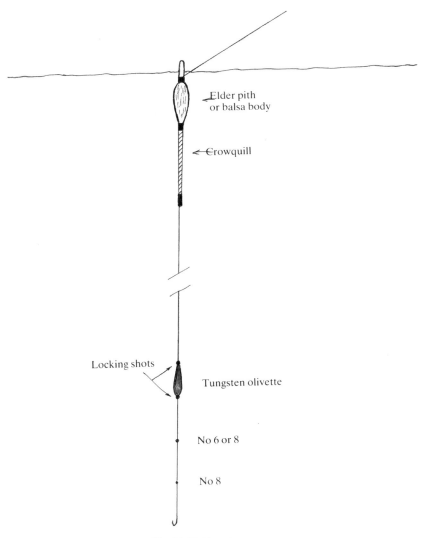

Elder pith
or balsa body

Crowquill

Locking shots

Tungsten olivette

No 6 or 8

No 8

Fig. 24. Fishing the Topper.

the bulk weight bouncing around lower down, if you try to open the
bale arm with your left hand whilst holding the rod in your right hand,
you will continually get tangles. You must always hold the rig in one
hand and cast with the other using a smooth underhand swing and this

Fig. 25. Casting a Topper.

can only be accomplished by using an automatic reel and I carry one around solely for these occasions (see Fig. 25). The only other type of float that I occasionally use is the all-balsa trotting float, but as Dave uses this pattern far more than I do I will let him explain.

Dave: I also carry around Toppers and use them much the same as Ken, but these days I think that the balsa float is very widely 'under used'. The number of occasions when using balsa, that I have had good bags of roach from what were seemingly empty pegs when using ordinary stick floats, is too numerous to mention.

I use them a lot in the winter months when the rivers are carrying extra water and some swims are deep with a lot of pace. In these conditions stick floats are totally wrong. I cannot see the point in using stick floats with strung out shots which will not settle until the tackle reaches the very end of the swim, when the fish are feeding in the bottom couple of feet of water. I carry balsa floats around with me from 3 B.B. right up to 7 A.A.A. but for most of my fishing I find I am using 5 or 6 B.B. capacity. The shotting pattern for a balsa is very, very simple: I usually have a No. 6 or a No. 8 just under the float, which I use purely as a depth marker. I then bunch 5 or 6 B.B. about 3 ft from the hook. Below this I might have one or two small droppers, sometimes a single

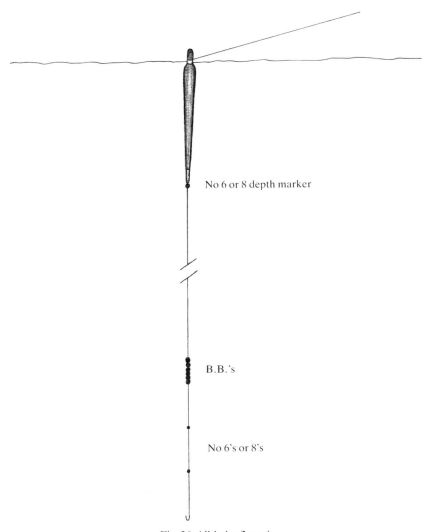

Fig. 26. All-balsa float rig.

No. 6 which I juggle around and on occasions can be as near as 6 or
8 inches to the hook, and sometimes this will be split up into a couple
of No. 8's. It is very seldom that I change from what is essentially a
very simple shotting pattern (see Fig. 26). The rig itself can be allowed

Fig. 27. A bait dropper.

to run through with the flow or checked and slowed down, putting it through slower than the current. You just need to keep experimenting until you find how the fish want the bait on the day. Sometimes under these conditions, there is no way you can get your loose feed down to the fish within the confines of your swim. On these occasions you will either have to use ground bait or loose feed with a bait dropper (see Fig. 27).

Ken: The Topper was originally designed for use on the Bristol Avon. In many places this river can be very deep and slow flowing and suffers from a problem not found on the majority of British rivers. Because it flows from East to West it has a prevailing 'upstream' wind. This means that on these deeper slower stretches the wind can prevent you from putting your bait through with the speed of the current using normal stick float tactics. But by having all of this weight concentrated several feet from the hook, the current has something to get hold of and it pulls it through the swim against the wind. It is very important to remember this for those odd occasions when you are faced with a strong upstreamer on the Trent or Thames, etc.

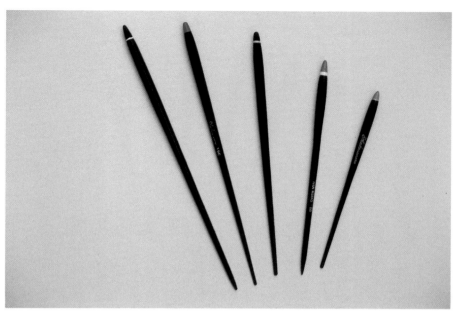

Traditional cane and balsa stick floats.

Bulbous stemmed lignum stick floats for long-range casting. Very popular with northern anglers.

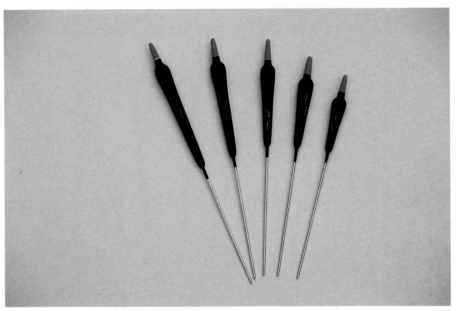

Shouldered wire stem floats. Ideal for holding back in winter conditions.

Wire stemmed and plastic stemmed stick floats.

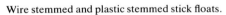

Medium capacity balsas used in heavier flows.

Ken's tray of stick floats.

Ken's range of Toppers.

Ken's tray of Wagglers.

Top quality bronze maggots: currently the modern match anglers top choice of bait.

Fresh casters: on the right day, the deadliest of all baits.

Releasing the clips at the bottom of the Steadfast Protectanet.

Fish being released out of bottom of net into the weighing net.

Feeding Methods and Tactics

Q. *How do you decide upon which baits to use and what would be your initial feeding tactics at the beginning of a match? How would these vary to suit the conditions, i.e. winter and summer, flood conditions and high and low water temperatures etc.?*

Dave: This goes hand in hand with what we talked about earlier with regards to doing your homework, so you know how much bait to take to a particular venue. This does not mean of course that you will use it all regardless, but you do need to know that if you have drawn on fish, you have enough bait to get you through the match and to respond to how well the fish are feeding. As to the type of baits, currently 90% of my fishing is done with bronze maggots because at the moment this is the match winning bait. Obviously this varies from area to area, but there are no hard and fast rules on this and again pre-match preparation, practice and information on the current form of the venue are the deciding factors. Whichever bait you take, it must be of the highest quality and you must have enough of it to do the job.

Many anglers, at the beginning of a match, make the mistake of feeding too heavily to start with. They have heard that the previous match was won with 20 or 30 lb and if they have drawn in a possible match winning area they start to feed with this target in mind. This is completely wrong. On many venues a match can be won one day with this weight, but in the next match, which may be on the following day, the winning weight may only be 7 or 8 lb, so this approach is totally wrong, as you are going to end up killing the swim off in the first half hour.

I always start off by feeding 10 to 15 maggots on each line per trot down the swim. I always feed at least two lines, and sometimes 3 or 4 on wider rivers, but always I will feed a waggler line and a line closer in where I can use a waggler or a stick float, depending upon conditions and try to judge from the response of the fish just what sort of a day it's going to be.

In the summer months most venues will take a lot more bait than in the winter. Fish of various sizes will be milling around at all different levels, with a lot of small fish just below the surface or at mid-depth, taking the bait on the drop and sometimes producing those fast unhittable bites that plague us all from time to time. Obviously under these circumstances, even if we are connecting with these smaller fish, a feed rate of 15 or 20 maggots will not be sufficient. This will only bring us 4 or 5 lb of fish over the course of the match and if the target weight is 20–30 lb then this approach needs to be modified. Gradually I would step up the amount of feed in an attempt to feed these smaller fish off and I would hope to be connecting with the larger fish by at least mid-match. If for example, a shoal of chub should move in, then I would probably use more bait over the period of the next half hour or so, providing the catch rate is maintained, than I had used in the first half of the match. On many occasions where I have got through a gallon of maggots by the end of the match, I may only have used one or two pints in the first 3 hours, the balance being used up when the better fish have moved into the swim in the last couple of hours and when I have put 20 lb plus into the net. Naturally, as well as changing the feeding pattern, I also have to alter my depth and presentation a number of times to get through the smaller fish and locate where the better fish are feeding. But often once the bigger fish do move in, especially chub, the smaller fish are bullied out of the swim anyway.

In the summer, I am looking to getting a much quicker response from the fish during the earlier part of the match and so I feed far more heavily than I would do during the winter.

During the winter months, when the smaller fish are far less active, I would start off as in summer with 10 to 15 maggots per trot. Hopefully I will pick up odd fish steadily throughout the match with a view to building up the swim for the last hour, particularly if the target species are roach. I would not increase the amount of feed until the fish move in and are feeding confidently and even then I would cut back to my original feed rate at the slightest slowing down of the bite rate.

You can get away with the odd feeding mistake in the summer months when there are plenty of fish to clean up the swim, but in winter you must always be on your guard to cut back when things slow down. Overfeed them and you will kill the swim for the rest of the match.

Ken: I remember recently when we had an important match on the Thames and where this point was dramatically brought home to us. We found in practice, that when we started to catch fish, if we increased the feed rate in response it killed the swim stone dead, which was surprising, as on such a big river with a strong rate of flow in the winter months, you would expect it to take a lot of bait and if a feeding mistake was made, the river would flush the excess away and you could correct it. But no, it killed the swim for the rest of the session. We found that on the day of the match we only needed to feed two pints over the course of the match and this had to be trickled in steadily and sparingly over the whole 5 hours. This just goes to show how important it is to practice, especially when you are going to fish a venue you are not very familiar with. You cannot take for granted that the methods you use regularly on your local venues will work for you on all rivers.

Dave has fully covered what is our 'basic' approach to feeding rates and how to adjust them in response to the fish. On most rivers this works, but you must always be prepared for the unexpected. Obviously, in the winter, especially after a sharp frost, you are not going to start blasting bait into the river. You will trickle it in sparingly and that 10 to 15 maggots may not go in all at the same time. You may feed 3 or 4 maggots three or four times during the course of your trot down, as opposed to all 15 at once.

Top anglers work on instinct and gut feelings which are very difficult to put into words. As Dave has said, in the summer months you expect some sort of response early on and after the first 15 or 20 minutes you have a good idea what sort of day it's going to be, provided of course that you have drawn a reasonable area and you are 'on' fish. You will have found out what species are present and in what sort of numbers and you make up your match from there. Most top match anglers are very adaptable and can jump either way from one species to another, feeding each line to suit the species present. They may have roach on their near line and chub or dace feeding on the waggler line. We will be talking about 'timing' your feeding later on, but when they actually switch tackle to fish one line opposed to another, they will automatically alter their feeding to suit the different species, steadily trickling feed down to the roach, or putting the hook bait down with a bunch of loose feed on the chub and dace line. Again it's all down to experience and practice.

Q. *Many anglers fail to appreciate the timing and position of their feeding. What points do you consider are essential and how do you plan your rhythm to ensure that your hookbait and loose feed are being synchronized to their maximum potential?*

Ken: I always prefer, where possible, to feed a swim slightly downstream particularly when fishing at close range. This helps to create an 'empty' area in front and slightly downstream of me. I think this is very important for two reasons. One, it allows me to cast in and have the tackle under complete control before it reaches the catching area, ensuring perfect presentation, and two, it means I am not bringing a hooked fish through

Ken Giles with his section-winning catch in the 1989 Old Holborn Classic which
won him second individual place.

the feeding shoal and unsettling them. To me, the worst thing that can happen is to have the fish feeding directly in front. You miss a lot of bites because you are unable to straighten out and control the tackle and you are unable to strike directly or smoothly. Also, if you do hook a fish you end up playing it out in the middle of the shoal which is all wrong. There is also the added disadvantage of course that the angler upstream is in a better position to bring the shoal of fish past you and up into his swim. So it is important, where possible, to feed slightly downstream. There are times of course when fishing in faster flows, that you need to feed slightly upstream, especially when the pegging is short, but you must keep an eye on where you are catching and if the fish appear to be moving up too close you must adjust the feed to make them move back down again. The feeding for the waggler is also dependent upon the flow and depth but unlike the stick float, where we look to be feeding in front or downstream, more often than not on the waggler, especially on the faster waters with some depth, we will be feeding well upstream of ourselves. We often have the situation on these types of waters, where we are feeding several yards upstream and catching fish 15 yards downstream of us.

Dave: I agree with Ken about the placing of the feed. As to the timing, except under exceptional circumstances, I tend to keep a steady trickle of feed going down the swim all of the time. I generally cast in and then feed three or four times or even more often on occasions during the course of the trot, the amount being dictated by the response of the fish and the time of the year, as we have already discussed. The exception to this is when I am chub or dace fishing on waters where the fish are particularly educated. Here it is important to feed and then cast in and draw the tackle over the feed as it goes through the swim, so that your hookbait is going through together with the bunch of loose feed. This is often the only way you will get bites, as these fish will often ignore a single offering but will dive into a bunch of maggots.

   If my usual feeding approach is not working as well as usual, I will vary it during the course of the match to see if it improves the catch rate. Again, you need to read what is happening and adjust things to suit the feeding habits of the various species. The important thing is to keep the feed going in on each line all of the time. Do not get so preoccupied with your catching line and forget your reserve lines. Get into the rhythm and keep it going.

Ken: Yes, generally, this is very important. By maintaining the feeding on the reserve line, even if you have not used it for an hour or so, if fish are present you are giving them confidence and when eventually you do need to switch lines, you know that if fish are there, they will respond

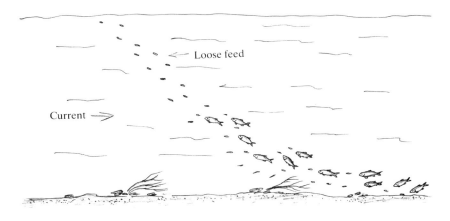

Fish rising in the water in response to loose feed.

within two or three trots down. If after two or three trots you do not get a bite, you can be confident that this is because there are no fish there yet and you can revert to your other line, but you must still keep those reserve lines fed for when the fish do move in. Normally it is usual to be able to take fish from both lines once they are established, on a regular basis and when this happens it is important that you do not finish either line out completely of fish. You need to leave each line with a few fish still feeding on it when you change. These will attract other fish into the swim and help them to settle down and feed confidently. The hardest thing to do is to attract fish into a completely barren area. It is hard to explain, but with experience you can sense when to rest a swim and switch lines, even though you know that the fish are still there and they can be caught. So you catch two or three from the stick float line, rest the swim and take two or three from the waggler line. By doing this, the fish you leave will attract more fish into the swim and given them the confidence to feed and settle down. This of course is the ideal situation providing that both swims play ball. But if you ever do empty a swim clean, that line will die and it can stay dead for the duration of the match.

Up to now we have assumed that we are fishing waters with a good head of hungry fish. There are times on certain venues such as the Upper Avon with a limited population of fish, where this approach will not work. If you are fishing a stick float line and regularly blast feed out to the waggler line, the fish on the far line will happily gobble up the free offerings and once they are full they will disappear. This means that when you eventually do go over to the waggler line, you are putting your bait through a swim full of contented fat bellied fish which have no inclination to consume any more feed. In these circumstances you must only feed the line you are actually fishing and of course you must expect it to take a little longer before you get a response when you change. Again it all comes back to local knowledge of a venue and experience. It's all very confusing isn't it?

Q. *There are times when you are catching well and the fish gradually move up the swim getting progressively closer and higher in the water and then suddenly the bites stop. How do you alter your rhythm to get back in touch with the fish and keep the catch rate going?*

Ken: Panic like bloody hell!

Dave: Yes, we certainly do!
This can be a combination of things. As Ken has already mentioned, a lot of anglers make the mistake, particularly on shallow water, of feeding too high up the swim. There is a real danger when fishing on shallow water of bringing the fish too close to you and two things can occur; the fish you are catching can disturb the fish who are waiting or moving up and you can end up with the fish in an uncatchable position. This happens a lot on waters such as the Upper Trent. They come right up under your feet and it's just impossible to present your bait properly. If you get into this situation you have got to get out of it as quickly as possible or there is a very real danger of losing your fish to the competitor upstream, because if he is doing his job right, he will take the fish off of you. I learnt this lesson very early on in my match fishing career on the Warwickshire Avon, where the very experienced angler above me actually took the fish off of me completely and it wasn't until the very last hour that I realised what he had done. I have done it to others many times since then and it is one of those very hard lessons that any match angler must learn if he intends to be successful. What actually happened on that day was this. I was probably on the match winning peg and I had taken one or two fish early on and I was content with just catching, as it was one of my very first matches. The angler above me was actually feeding down the swim as well as in front of him and for no apparent reason I just stopped catching after about an hour. He went on to win the match with around 20 lb and I ended up with only about 7 lb, mostly of which I had taken early on. I still honestly think that on the day I had the match winning peg but due to my inexperience and being unable to realise what was happening, I blew it. When bites stop it can be a variety of things that are happening. It might be that the peg is just not good enough to provide a win and you have exhausted it. If the bites have dried up and you feel that you have fed

it correctly, then you would look to fishing further out, changing if necessary from the stick float to the waggler and gradually feeding one to two rod lengths further out, but still feeding the original line in case the fish get confident and start feeding later on. You must keep experimenting at that stage, by altering your depth and the rate of fall of your tackle, ease back on the feed, you may have overfed it, or in some circumstances increase the feed, you may not have given them enough. You must keep experimenting and even if you do not find the fish again you can at least content yourself with the fact that you tried your hardest and the swim on the day was not a winning peg.

Q. *When reading match reports and articles on match fishing, the term 'building up' a swim is mentioned, but never fully explained. Many club level anglers panic if bites are not forthcoming in the first half hour of a match, yet many top river anglers seem unconcerned and even suggest that on occasions this can sometimes be a good sign and have the confidence to stick it out and steadily build up the catch rate. We lesser mortals on the other hand try to make the most of the bites when they do come, but often find ourselves struggling in the last couple of hours, whilst anglers of your calibre are catching at an ever increasing rate. Where are we going wrong?*

Ken: Many times you plan for catching during the latter part of the match but the planning is unintentional. It's just the way things turn out. Obviously the majority of anglers, ourselves included, would prefer to catch fish right from the very first cast up until the very last cast, but unfortunately this situation doesn't occur very often. A good match angler knows that if he can be in touch with the fish for just a couple of hours during the 5 hours of a match, and that providing they are of the match winning species such as chub or quality roach, he has the ability and confidence to know that he stands a good chance of winning. If he does not catch early on he will not be unduly worried. He will have spent the first hour trimming his tackle to suit the conditions, getting his floats going through the swim properly and under control during the maximum period of the trot and he will have adjusted his feeding so that when the fish do eventually move in, he has everything working right and can concentrate upon having a killing time whilst the fish are there and feeding. A lot depends upon the time of the year. During the summer months the fish could come on the feed at any time during the match, but in the winter it is often in the last hour that the fish start to feed and many anglers plan their match for this and this is why they say at the end of a match, that because they had a good burst of chub or a good burst of roach in that last hour, it has won them the match. This is of course down to confidence and the knowledge that this is the

Fig. 28. Ken preparing to net an Avon chub at Twyfords Farm.

period when the fish will start to feed and they have prepared the swim and the tackle properly beforehand.

The worst thing you can do at this time of year is to feed out of habit, as opposed to in response to the fish. Lean times mean lean feeding. If you just ladle the feed in regardless every run down during the first 4 hours whilst you are not catching, you will kill the swim for the duration.

The reason why some anglers panic if they do not start to catch early on is because they doubt their own ability. If you know you are doing everything right and have confidence in your ability, you will not get worried and you will take it as it comes, knowing that if the fish start to respond you are ready. If at the end of the match the fish do not come on and you blank, which happens to the best of us on occasions, you can accept that you have done everything right and that you did not get the draw on the day.

Dave: One of the key factors to it all is work rate. I often see on many matches I have been on, where everybody starts off on the float using either the stick or the waggler or eventually alternating with both and after a fruitless hour or so, one by one the feeder rods or the straight leger rods come out and you can see that they have given up on the work rate and take what they consider to be the easier option. Not only have they given up on the method, but they have also stopped feeding their float fishing lines and for my part I love to see it when the angler below does that. It gives me an open licence to not only have my fish when they come on, but his fish as well. The secret is, by all means try another method if nothing at all is happening at that stage, but don't completely give up. Keep some sort of regular feed rate going in on the original lines. By doing this you give yourself an option to go back on it later on. If you fail to do this and then two hours later the angler above you suddenly starts to catch on the float, there is no way you can go back on it and hope to catch him up again.

I think that work rate is the key to it all. The key to everything we have spoken about so far. You must keep going. Keep changing the shotting and depth, the feeding pattern etc, keep working and look for areas in the peg that can give you the best return.

Ken: Could I just add a little bit more at this stage? You will find that the good anglers will keep feeding all their lines right up to the very last cast, even though in the last hour they have been catching well, say on the stick float line. The reason is this, if by any chance there is an accident in the last 5 or ten minutes, i.e. you crack off above the float or pull out a fish and get an almighty tangle, you know that instead of wasting time trying to rig up again that you can throw that rod up the bank and take hold of the waggler rod and go out on the reserve line and still be participating in the match. By doing this you know that the line is still alive and you may take a couple more fish in those last few minutes which could make the difference between winning or being second or even out of the frame.

Dave: Just going back to the original question about building up the swim. It is a misconception that you are always building it up for that last hour. In the winter it does tend to be that in the last hour or hour and a half the swim does happen to be at its most productive, but in the summer months it may be that you just happen to be building it up for a good middle hour. All of a sudden you could get a shoal of chub move in and before you know where you are you could have put 20 lb in the net. After that the swim dies again and you may not have a bite in the last two hours, but you may have caught enough in that middle period to win. If, on the other hand, you have given up in the first hour and put your rod down and gone on to something else and stopped feeding all of your lines, then this building up process will have collapsed and you will have missed a possible match winning opportunity. As Ken has said, the building up process is actually taken up in the first hour or hour and a half and the rest of the match is taken up from there.

Q.   *I would now like to discuss 'GAMESMANSHIP'. On several occasions when there have been no big matches on our local calendar, some of the local 'cracks' come on our club matches as spare riders and often bag up. Many of our club members bemoan the fact that they are unable to buy a bite, whilst the 'cracks' drawn at the side of them are emptying their own swim and theirs as well. How do you go about bringing up fish from neighbouring swims and slowing down their catch rate when they are out-performing you? Also, what precautions can you take to prevent them from doing the same to you?*

Dave: You've got a couple of options, you either ban the 'cracks' from coming on your club match or learn from what has happened. I would imagine the club anglers have gone back moaning about what's happened, but haven't analysed the situation and learnt from it. As I pointed out earlier, in one of my early matches this happened to me, when the angler above drew the fish from me. But I learnt from the experience and it was a lesson well learnt and whilst I have done it to many other anglers since, I have been determined that it wouldn't happen again to me. This situation tends to happen when an angler stops working. For example, he starts on the waggler then changes over to the stick float and forgets to keep feeding the waggler line. If there are a few fish still flying about in the second or third hour the chances are I will have his fish as well. If I am given this wonderful situation, I will fire a few maggots well downstream but still within the confines of my own swim, in the hope of drawing a few more of his fish up into my own swim.

As to stopping the angler below from catching, I do not like doing this and do not do it, because the volume of bait I would need to put in will not only kill his swim but my own as well. By all means, try to bring the fish past him by feeding sensibly downstream but never at the expense of killing his sport as well as your own. If the angler below is doing his job right and has got the better peg then good luck to him. You will achieve nothing by spoiling it for him and yourself, other than to say you were not pegged next to the winner. This is a very negative attitude and certainly not one that I condone.

Ken: I have to go along with that. There are certain people who we know are well known stoppers and to me it is just not sportsman-like. If the chap below has done his job right and has beaten you fair and square, then all you can do is get off of your basket at the end of the match and shake him by the hand and congratulate him on his performance. In this way you make friends rather than enemies and you need as many friends as possible on the circuit if you want to succeed. Remember what I said earlier on about ringing around for up to date information on a venue. No one is going to help you if you have alienated yourself by being unsporting and you will also miss out on a lot of post-match discussion back at the pub when a lot of information and detail about what has happened during the day is flying about. You can often learn more after the match over a few pints than you can by practising alone and if you make yourself a social outcast you will miss out on an awful lot.

Dave: People will never condemn you for bringing up fish providing you have played by the rules and you have done it fair and square. I remember one situation whilst fishing a match on the river Thames which amplifies this point.

I got to my peg in good time and on the way up I noticed a big shoal of chub basking in the rushes on the far bank about three pegs downstream. As it turned out, it was a hard day with only a few odd gudgeon and small roach being taken and one by one the two anglers downstream of me packed up and went home. To be honest, I felt like doing the same as it was a cold hard day and nothing much was happening. The angler who was pegged on the chub was not catching and was I believe fishing over the far side on a swimfeeder but was not connecting with the fish. Now that I had two empty pegs below me I started to catapult a few maggots right downstream on the far side and after half an hour or so the fish gradually moved up and the next hour was incredible. I caught chub after chub and finished off by weighing in 36½ lb. Instead of using 24 hooks to ¾ lb bottoms as I had been doing, I ended up using 2 lb line straight through to a size 16 hook. I was very fortunate that the two anglers below me had packed up. If the angler below me on the next peg had been in the same mind and stuck it out it might have happened to him and he may have won the match.

Ken: Sometimes on wide rivers, you can draw the other angler's fish up by fishing on a different line to the ones he is feeding. But on narrow rivers, particularly when the pegging is tight, it pays for you all to fish the same line, feeding the swim for the man downstream. There is one venue we fish where the pegging is particularly tight and where this is the unwritten rule. You trot your float a few yards into the next peg and we all feed for each other and it works. But it only needs one man in the chain to do it wrong and to feed too much, or too little and that mucks it up for everybody else. But generally everyone knows what the score is and we all work for each other, which let's face it, is what angling should be all about: sportsmanship.

In normal match situations, the only way of making sure your fish are not taken is to keep up the feeding on all your lines and as we have previously discussed, start putting your feed further downstream if the fish start to come up the swim too far.

Q. *What part does the use of groundbait play when float fishing on rivers and when do you use it? How do you know when its right to do so and what type of mix do you generally use?*

Ken: Here in the Midlands the waters tend to respond the best to loose feeding tactics and we seldom use groundbait. But having said that in recent seasons more people are using groundbait on occasions, than they ever used to do. This is mainly due to the introduction of specialist products from the continent and I must give this man his due, MARCEL VAN DEN EYNDE, who in particular, has revolutionised the British approach to groundbaiting with his vast range of products and knowledge. As someone who has experienced the groundbaiting era of the sixties and seventies, when its use was restricted to just brown or white breadcrumb mix, I can appreciate that in comparison to what's available now it just wasn't in the same class and you can only thank these people on the continent for making us aware of it. By now having all these different mixes to suit the individual species and conditions it has made us aware that there is much more to groundbait than the basic use of just white or brown breadcrumb that we always accepted as being groundbait.

As far as using it on flowing water is concerned, it is mainly down to the various species present. Bream often respond well to its careful use, as do roach on occasions. But for dace and chub it is usually the

This catch of quality bream and carp gave Ken Giles second place in the Arrow Valley Lakes Championship.

kiss of death as generally they do not seem to like it very much. The depth and flow of water is also a key factor. In some places where you have 10 or 12 ft of water and a good head of responsive fish such as bream, then it can be very useful for getting the bait down within the confines of the swim and holding them there. But on shallower venues with a variety of mixed species, until we have a fuller understanding of the various qualities and ingredients, then we tend to rely on the proven effectiveness of loose feeding.

Dave: Yes, I have to agree. We are in the middle of a learning process with these new products and its use at the moment is mainly restricted to practice sessions or venues where it has a proven effect. I had a reasonable degree of success with it on the Trent last summer (89). I have been using a 50–50 mix of Van Den Eynde Super Cup and Secret in conjunction with caster feed. I found it to be very versatile and I could get the perfect mix for any given type of swim. I could mix it soft or I could mix it hard and I did have a lot of success. I have also experimented with it on the Warwickshire Avon and I have had some startling results at times, but the hardest thing in the world is to draw a good peg and to start firing in groundbait when you know you have a good chance of winning the match with traditional loose feed tactics. You just cannot afford to take the risk. But I remember one incident at a match on the Avon at Twyfords where I drew not too badly, not one of the hot pegs but just off of them, and it was one of those days when the fish were completely switched off to loose fed maggots. Nobody could get a bite, three hours into the competition, I had one chub in the net about 12 oz and nothing seemed to be moving. I went for a walk and established that the best weight on the entire length was only about 5 lb. So I went back to my peg and it was apparent, because we knew the fish were there, that loose fed maggots would not do the trick then as it was a warm summer's day and the venue had received a lot of pressure over the previous weeks. So I made up a bowl of groundbait with Secret and Super Cup and a bit of crushed hemp and mixed it up fairly softly, put a few casters in and fed a couple of very soft balls over with the catapult. I was only fishing about 3 or 4 ft deep, suddenly a shoal of chub moved in and in the next hour I went on to take just over 15 lb and came second to a 16 lb weight from the top end of the match. So I went back down again a couple of days later, only this time to a better peg, fished exactly the same mix under similar conditions and I couldn't get a bite!

So as you see we are very much in an experimental stage. We are all trying it and learning from each other but as yet have not reached any definite conclusions.

Ken: As I have already said, from an older angler's point of view, I have been through the era where everybody used groundbait. No matter where you were fishing, or for what species, you always used groundbait. During the Billy Lane era everyone used to take 20 lb or more of white groundbait with them to a match and the lot would go in. Then we had the period when people switched to brown crumb to try to get an advantage and eventually when that was blown we came into the loose feed era. What is happening now is that these new products are coming onto the market and naturally they have to be looked at, as it is possible that once we understand the way that the various ingredients act together to attract and stimulate the feeding response of the fish, we will be able to use them to our advantage. The continentals of course are years ahead of us in this department. You go into tackle shops abroad and there are rooms full of different ingredients which they use to make up their various mixes and they have a much better understanding of the qualities of the ingredients needed to suit certain species and venues. But slowly we are coming to realise that there is something in it and we are all beginning to experiment. I think that if you were to ask this question again in a couple of years time you would get a far more positive answer. But until then not only do we need to experiment, but we need to break down the psychological barrier that is preventing us from taking advantage of the knowledge as we develop. As Dave has already said, there is the problem of drawing a peg with a loose feed potential of 20 lb and by putting in groundbait you may kill it. But at the same time by not doing that you will never know if by using groundbait you can increase its potential to 35 or 40 lb.

Dave: What we need to know with continental groundbaits is the way that *they* fish with it. Admitted, in France the emphasis is on its use with bloodworms, but in Holland it is used in conjunction with more conventional baits which is why as maggot and caster anglers we are drawn more to the Dutch and Belgian formulas as opposed to the French.

To our advantage we have lots of loose feed readily available from tackle shops such as maggots, casters and squatts etc., but due to the European restrictions they do not have the same amount of loose feed available, so they tend to concentrate far more with the use of what we can only loosely term as groundbait. I can recall fishing a match in Holland in 1985. I watched a famous angler preparing to fish a match on the North Sea Canal there and he made up about 30 balls of groundbait mix, the size of which I have never seen before; something like cannon balls, and it smelt good enough to eat. I was watching him as he mixed it up and into it he only put something like the equivalent of half pint of pinkies. Now for that volume of groundbait it was a drop in the ocean, so it was apparent that it was the groundbait that he was intending to work for him. He had a fantastic number of different ingredients in there such as crushed nuts etc, and it did really smell appetizing. Anyway to cut a long story short, all he used was this mix, with half pint of pinkies and a red maggot on the hook and he went on to take about 20 lb of bream. So somewhere between this approach and our approach with loose feed there must be a balance, if we can eventually arrive at it. As things stand at the moment, with the prospect of those same EEC regulations restricting maggot production in this country as well, we may also be forced into using groundbait in the same way.

Q. *Bait preparation plays an important part of your pre-match activities and the use of additives of various types are now very popular. In recent sessions our own club's bus smells like a cross between a delicatessen and an abattoir. What importance do you attach to the use of bait additives and how do you go about preparing your bait?*

Ken: Normally, for the majority of my river fishing, I use plain bronze maggots, full stop. If I am going on a bream venue, I would breed my own gozzers to be used as a hook bait in conjunction with commercial bronze maggots as the loose feed. As far as the use of additives is concerned on loose baits, I don't use any. I have tried them but they do not seem to do anything for me. There doesn't seem to be a definite yes or no as to whether they serve any purpose or not. I wouldn't doubt it that in groundbait they might serve a purpose, but I cannot see the point of using them on loose bait. If it gives a person confidence then so be it, let them use it, but for my part I have not found any advantage in their use. I must admit that I like to use turmeric on my bait, but not for attraction purposes. I have found that turmeric does dispel a lot of the grease from the maggots and helps them to sink faster through the water. This at times gives a positive advantage, so in these circumstances I use it, but to my mind the use of additives as attractors are a non-starter and there is no substitute for a fresh clean maggot properly presented by the angler. Too much effort is wasted in chasing these rainbows, hoping to find some sort of magic formula. There is just no substitute for ability and anglers should concentrate their efforts upon improving their techniques.

Dave: My approach is exactly the same really, I do believe in getting good quality bait. I may have 4 or 5 pints of maggots in my fridge, but if they are more than a few days old I will always go out and buy fresh bait for use in a match. I don't believe in using old bait at all, even in the winter; despite all the articles that have been written about older maggots not stretching as much in cold conditions. I may take a handful with me for occasional use on the hook, but I am a big believer in having the biggest, freshest maggots I can get. If I could get it direct from the farm I would, but fortunately I do have a good tackle shop that supplies me with good quality bait and I am quite happy with it. I have experimented this season with using various attractors and like Ken I can find no advantage in them. I am also a big believer in turmeric for the same reasons that Ken has pointed out and I do still use chrysodine dye.

I think the controversy over its use is wrong. This is my personal opinion after reading things and seeing things etc., but I do still use it where it is allowed. Where it is not allowed, as I do not like any of the new dyes being used, I would just use a turmeric coloured maggot.

Let us say for instance that I buy 6 pints of maggots. When I get them home I will riddle them off and get rid of all the rubbish so I am left with just straight clean maggots. Onto these I would sprinkle a small amount of dry chrysodine powder, put them in the fridge and within an hour or so that dye will have taken on to the maggots. I would then take half a pint to one side and put them in a separate container and leave them on the dye for the whole of the night. I then add a few handfuls of maize meal to the other 5½ pints and leave that in the fridge separate. The next morning I will put the half pint, which by now would be very dark bronze, back with the other maggots, riddle them through and add another couple of handfuls of fresh maize meal plus a bit of turmeric as well. Sometimes, if I get chance I will do the same just before the match, again adding fresh turmeric. By doing this I get very clean bait and do not have the problem of the excess dye coming off all over my hands. The half pint that has been left longer on the dye make nice dark hookbaits which the fish, especially the roach, find very attractive. I also have a scoop of red maggots and disco maggots, which are very popular in our area and add these to the bait as well, because quite often during the latter part of the match, by using one of these on the hook as a change you can get the odd couple of extra bites.

Q. *Many matchmen consider the use of hempseed essential due to its un-questionable fish holding qualities. How do you use it and in what sort of quantity? Are there any occasions when you find its introduction detrimental?*

Ken: Recently the Italian match angler Milo Columbo came to Evesham on several occasions and each time he only drew what were considered mediocre pegs. He loose fed hempseed alone and just used a single maggot on the hook. On each occasion he caught what we consider to be a reasonable weight from the pegs he drew.

For the people who don't know Evesham, it is a very hard-fished water and for someone to come from abroad, to see it for the first time and put it all together is quite an achievement. It is a pity he did not draw one of the good pegs so we could have seen how well he did in those in comparison to their normal form.

I do use hempseed a lot, in what I consider to be a reasonable quantity and I always take some with me to a match, although I may not use it on every occasion.

It is a good holding bait, it sinks quickly and once it is on the bottom it stays there. It doesn't get washed away downstream like maggots and casters. During the summer months I will use it in conjunction with my normal loose feed, but sometimes in the winter, when water temperatures are very low, I will feed just hempseed on its own, using a maggot or caster on the hook. I know the fish are unlikely to be eating it, but this is an advantage, as they will get interested in anything falling through the water and will possibly have a go at my hook bait without filling up on the loose feed.

With regards to its use as a hook bait, although you can get good catches with it in practice, it is seldom that it performs in matches. Why I don't know, but having said that I remember coming 5th or 6th in a National Championship Match on the Nene using hempseed on the hook. I drew a peg which we had practiced on the week before and had caught well on hempseed, so as soon as I saw where I was I thought 'Well, I will give it a try'. So I put a bit in and within a short space of time I was catching roach. But normally I only use it as an attractor.

Dave: Generally, I only use hempseed in the summer and autumn. To be truthful I don't often carry hemp in the winter months at all. I just use maggots or casters. But I have witnessed anglers using up to two gallons of hempseed in pursuit of barbel on the Severn during just one session and having done it myself and seen the results, I am totally convinced that they are dead right in this approach for that particular species. I wouldn't dream of going to a match on the Middle Severn in summer without taking at least 6 pints of it with me and complement that with 5 or 6 pints of casters as well. It's a wild river and they are very hungry fish, so to compete you do need this amount of bait.

On the Warwickshire Avon, the Trent, the Nene and venues such as this, I would probably take about three pints with me in the summer and fish this in conjunction with caster. But there is sometimes the very real problem of the fish becoming totally preoccupied with the hempseed if you over do it and then you are struggling. There are days when you are using the stick float with traditional shotting patterns, where you are plagued with shot bites and even if you are using hemp on the hook you are only hitting about one in six of the bites; you are in the silly situation of getting the fish feeding madly but cannot catch enough to win. I love to use hempseed in the summer months and especially when I can use it in conjunction with tares as well. But seed baits are funny things to use at the best of times and although you can have glorious sport in practice, they seldom perform under match conditions. But I don't think there is ever any danger in putting hemp into a swim unless you over do it, apart from the Severn, where you do need to put a lot in.

Match Experiences

Q. *Finally, to try to put some of the points we have covered into perspective I would like you to think back and tell me about any particular match, successful or otherwise, where you had to work really hard and make a lot of changes and adjustments to find and keep in touch with the fish, explaining what you had to do and why you did it. Also where appropriate, what mistakes you may have made and in hindsight, how you could have perhaps improved upon your final result.*

Dave: I've got two matches I would like to talk about, one, where I almost fished a perfect match and the other, where thanks to the response of the fish, I actually think I did.

As practising match anglers we are always striving to improve upon our performance and fish what we think is a perfect match. In 1986 I fished a competition at Shrewsbury on the river Severn and I drew two pegs below the toll bridge on the quarry length.

It was apparent that the river was rising at the start of the match, and this confirmed the information I had received by ringing up the river report service that morning. It had been rising since the previous day, so I was half expecting it to be bank high. When I actually saw the river, I was pleasantly surprised to find that it was still at a good fishing level despite the extra water.

I started off by fishing a waggler down the middle of the river, in the full knowledge that the river would be rising during the course of the match. I fed steadily and after about an hour I started to catch roach and I probably had these fish going for about ¾ of an hour before the river came up and coloured up too much to keep catching on that particular line.

I had also been feeding steadily throughout this period close in on the stick float line, so I switched to that and almost immediately started to catch on that line as well. I caught fairly steadily over the next couple of hours but with about an hour of the match still to go, it became more and more difficult to put the tackle through properly as the water was now beginning to boil and swirl on the surface and got very coloured and my bites stopped altogether. I put my float rod behind me and started to fish with a straight leger rod which I had made up at the start of the match in anticipation of these conditions arising, and continued to catch two or three fish in the last half an hour from what was previously my stick float line. At the end of the day I came second in the match with 14 lb 15 oz, beaten by a weight of 15 lb 6 oz from a peg higher upstream. After I had finished I thought I had fished a perfect match with regards to the conditions, but I came second and in hindsight, I feel that if I had fed heavier at the start of the match to get a quicker response on the waggler, I would have got those few extra fish out of the waggler line before it became impossible to fish and they probably would have won the match. The trend at Shrewsbury and on other parts of the Severn, is to feed steady, but on this day, because I was only going to be able to fish that line for part of the match, I should have fed heavier for a quicker response.

But last season (he says modestly), I fished what I consider to have been the perfect match. There was a lot of pressure hanging upon it as I was lying second in the Angler's Mail Matchman of the Year league and 4 points behind the then leader. We had only two matches to go, one on the Saturday and one on the Sunday, so I was under a lot of pressure to get a result. On the Saturday I went to Twyford farm on the Warwickshire Avon, and as I recall there were over 100 anglers fishing the match, and I drew peg 69 on what we call 'the straight'. It's a good peg for a few roach, but it is not a noted peg to win from, as it was not in a winning area. So a lot was going through my mind such as 'Where was the other angler ahead of me in the league drawn?' and 'Can I get enough fish out of the peg to get into the top 4 and gain some points?' I came to the conclusion that I must work extremely hard, feeding and fishing a number of lines, if I was to get enough fish out of the swim to stand a chance.

So I set up a variety of rigs. I set up a 3 A.A.A. waggler, a 5 no. 4 stick float and a 14 metre pole rig.

I started off by feeding three appropriate lines for the three different methods and started by fishing the waggler on the far bank. I was fortunate to catch a few chub early on plus a few roach and I had caught 4 or 5 lb in the first hour and a half. Bites were beginning to slow and I sensed that it was time to rest that line, so I switched to the stick float and started going down the side, just off the end of the landing stage and caught another 2 or 3 lb of roach before my bites stopped again. As I have mentioned, all the time I had been feeding a third line in mid-river with a view to using the pole, and when I went out on this I also started to catch a few fish on that line as well, and over the course of the last two hours of the match things went absolutely perfectly. We do not very often have perfect situations. We would all like to fish an ideal match, where we feed two or three lines and keep on catching from each one in turn, all of the way through the match. Unfortunately these are the exception as opposed to the normal, but on this day it worked like a dream and everything I tried worked for me. I was talking to some lads whilst I was fishing towards the end of the match and I remember telling them that I was having a good match, catching steadily and not losing many fish, but deep down I knew I needed that little bit more. In the latter part of the match in the last ¾ of an hour, I started to feed pretty heavily across the river in pursuit of what I thought I needed which was two or three chub to swing the match my way. I will always recall commenting to these lads 'If I can only get a couple of chub now, that will seal it'. And it was as if the heavens had opened up and god had looked down and said 'OK Dave', because I picked the waggler rod up for the last 10 minutes and had three chub, all in excess of 1 lb in weight. I ended up by winning the match with just under 18 lb and I think to this day that that was my perfect match, not only because the fish responded to everything that I did, but also because I did it dead right and gave the fish what they wanted as well. Obviously, by my past results I have fished some good matches, but I don't think I have ever fished a better one, especially considering the amount of pressure I was under to get a result.

Ken: One match that sticks in my memory was also a match where I came second, but unlike Dave's it was far from perfect with regards to how I approached it.

It was the 1989 Businessman's Open on the River Severn at Stourport. I drew what appeared to be a reasonable looking swim. The only problem was that there was a lot of boil on the inside. I set up a stick float, a waggler and a topper, rigged as usual with a tungsten olivette about 3 ft from the hook with a couple of droppers and almost immediately I started to catch one or two fish. Suddenly, I hit into a barbel of about 1 lb, and I thought to myself 'Yes, there are a few good fish here' and I kept plugging away. In the meantime I had been feeding the waggler line in mid-river, but because I had caught this barbel down the side I kept on fishing with the topper, despite the fact that my bites had stopped. Eventually, much later than I should have done, I switched to the waggler. I found I had about 14 ft out on the waggler line and eventually established that a few roach were feeding right on the bottom, so, I was struggling to cast this waggler out at full depth and with plenty of weight down the line. In 20 minutes or so I took a couple of roach, but then the line died and this barbel kept coming back into my mind. So I switched back again to the inside line with the topper. After a while I caught a chub and this made me persevere with the topper for another hour.

Eventually out of frustration and with about two hours of the match to go, I tried again with the waggler and those roach were there, queuing up for my bait. They were quality roach and I ended up weighing in 21 lb. Mark Downes won the match with 26 lb.

My mistake had been to persevere with the topper for far too long. To some degree I had given up on the work rate as Dave has mentioned. Casting and fishing the waggler at 14 ft was hard work and this early barbel had haunted me all the way through the match. If I had gone back and kept working on that waggler line a lot earlier, I feel certain that I could have had another 7 or 8 lb of those big roach out of the swim and have won the match.

I also recall a very recent match on the same venue, where I was forced to abandon the traditional float fishing methods and resort to heavy legering tactics with big baits, to fish my way back into the match. I did not win it, but I did come 5th and in the prize money from a no-hope peg. I know we are primarily concerned with float fishing methods, but I feel that this story does put over the essential point that we do not always draw the ideal peg for float fishing, but as matchmen, we still have to try to get a result. When things are really hard, it can pay to go completely opposite to the normal trend of using ultra fine hooks and lines with small baits to induce a few bites.

On this particular match, again at Stourport, I drew one peg below what is known as Gladder Brook. The river was carrying something like 18 inches of extra water. Now with 18 inches of extra water on the River Severn you can, at times catch a lot of fish, but due to the nature of the venue at Stourport, 18 inches of water causes a lot of problems. The river is lined with a lot of overhanging beech trees with roots going right out into the river. Under normal conditions you can put a float through comfortably just past these roots, but when the river is carrying this extra water there are very few pegs where you can put a float through properly without being continually snagged on these roots. Unfortunately under these conditions the fish are generally feeding right on the bottom, so you need to fish full depth if you are to catch.

I set up a float rod and put the float through successfully a couple of times without snagging, so I thought 'Great, we should get a few roach here'. Now the roach at Stourport are superb fish. Many of them run to around 1½ to 1¾ lb apiece. They really are big fish, so a dozen or so of these and you have a very good weight indeed.

I also set up a leger rod with 5 lb mainline and a 3 lb hook length, with the intention of starting off the match on the luncheon meat for the first hour, but feeding the near line with maggots and switching over to the float after an hour with the intention of catching some of these big roach. If in the meantime I could pick up a bonus chub or barbel on the leger, all well and good. After an hour on the leger I'd had no bites, so as planned, I switched over to the float and started to fish down the side.

It soon became apparent that those first couple of trots down the swim had been flukes. Almost every trot down I became snagged on these beech tree roots and after I had gone through a dozen hooks in almost as many minutes I realised I was on a no-hope peg as far as catching roach was concerned, so I went back onto the leger rod. I was using 2½ oz of lead to hold out where I wanted to, casting up-stream and jerking a few pieces of bait off to feed the swim. I was using flakes of luncheon meat on a size 4 hook, which must sound terrible to many match anglers, but I realised that this was the only way of fishing myself back into the match.

Anyway to cut a long story short, I finished up with two barbel, two chub and a roach and weighed in just under 10 lb. The match was won with 13 lb and I came 5th. The barbel weighed in between 3 to 4 lb apiece so I only needed one more good barbel and I could have won. This, I hope, illustrates how on occasions you can, by using big fish methods, put yourself back into the match from a no-hope situation. It is a gamble of course, but there is no way I could have caught anywhere near that weight by staying on the float in that particular swim, so I had nothing to lose by it.

Although I used the leger on this occasion, there are times when it pays to float fish a big bait such as bread flake, luncheon meat or worms, to attract bites from the big fish if you think they are in the swim but are not interested in smaller baits such as maggots and casters.

BEWARE

OVERHEAD ELECTRIC POWER LINES

WARNING!

Living for fishing is one thing. Dying for it, or maiming yourself for life, is quite another. The one blot on the history and development of pole fishing in the last decade has been the number of serious accidents involving poles and overhead power lines.

The new carbon poles are frighteningly efficient at conducting electricity. They are long enough nowadays to make contact with power lines, but they do not even need to connect. Get one near enough and the power arcs across, with devastating results.

Fellow anglers have been killed. Two friends of ours have been horribly burned, and one has lost part of a leg. It should never have happened; it cannot happen to you or to us? But of course it can, unless you and we take the greatest of care.

So obey warning notices, and the advice from the electricity generating industry and the National Federation of Anglers to LOOK OUT and LOOK UP whenever you even think about setting up pole tackle in an area you are not familiar with.

Perhaps the reason why "lightning" never strikes twice is that it does not usually have to....

PLEASE DON'T DIE FOR YOUR FISHING!